THE SOUL OF

PITTSBURGH

Essays on Life, Community and History

ED SIMON

THE
History
PRESS

Published by The History Press
Charleston, SC
www.historypress.com

Copyright © 2024 by Edward Simon
All rights reserved

Front cover: Ron Donoughe, *Spring Hill-City View*, 9″ × 12″ oil on panel, 2014. *Courtesy Senator John Heinz History Center, Special Collections Gallery.*

First published 2024

Manufactured in the United States

ISBN 9781467157315

Library of Congress Control Number: 2024930890

Notice: The information in this book is true and complete to the best of our knowledge. It is offered without guarantee on the part of the author or The History Press. The author and The History Press disclaim all liability in connection with the use of this book.

Europe stretches to the Alleghenies, America lies beyond.
—Ralph Waldo Emerson

They are my people and this is my town and it does my heart good just to be here.
—Art Rooney Sr.

CONTENTS

TO WRITE A HISTORY OF PITTSBURGH IS TO WRITE A HISTORY OF AMERICA

When I returned to Pittsburgh almost twenty years ago, before leaving again and then coming back again, I found myself being berated about my hometown's supposed provincialism by an unpleasant and obscenely rich man-child from Manhattan while we were at an impromptu brunch in Pamela's Diner. Following an orientation session for graduate students at Carnegie Mellon, a small group of us made our way down Forbes Avenue, and he, unfortunately, joined us. In my recollection, he was a juvenile forty, twitchy and there to pursue a master's degree in something like entertainment technology or technological entertainment. Though he repeatedly emphasized his private school education, his degree from one of the minor Ivies and his father's home in Southern California, the detail that most stands out in my mind was his crossing the street to retrieve a Starbucks after he found Pamela's coffee to be lacking. Within the first five minutes of eating pancakes, he explained that his parents were paying his rent on a two-bedroom in the Pennsylvanian, a luxury apartment at the edge of downtown in the former Union Station, a magnificent Victorian Beaux Arts terra-cotta building with a massive rotunda featuring inlaid stained glass. Living within the presence of all that past wealth—made by those responsible for the steel and glass canyons of his own youth—made no impression on him; having been in Pittsburgh for less than a week, he insulted the Pittsburgh Symphony Orchestra, the local art scene and the city's restaurants (including Pamela's, which serves America's greatest breakfast). He rendered his verdict— Pittsburgh was simply the "Paris of Appalachia."

To be a Pittsburgher is to cringe at the contradiction of having a triumphant pride in your city combined with embarrassment about how it is sometimes viewed. Pride because for all of its problems (and they're legion), you know how gorgeous Pittsburgh is; at the same time, you're also aware that it has frequently been a punchline to those who have never been here, both before and after the economic collapse of the 1980s that nearly destroyed us. My man-child's quip wasn't uncommon, but it's become less frequent as, for better and worse, the city's cultural capital has risen. After the hundredth comeback article in the *New York Times* along the lines of "Pittsburgh Thrives After Casting Steel Aside" or "Built on Steel, Pittsburgh Now Thrives on Culture," the old jokes appear much less often. But this means that one simplistic media portrayal—Pittsburgh as a blue-collar shot-and-a-beer town—has been replaced with an equally simplistic revision, in which city leaders wouldn't mind being known as an organic quinoa and microbrew hamlet (or whatever), a type of Portland on the Mon.

Any media narrative is bound to lose something, and yet, I suspect any Pittsburgher sees in these conventional stories something reductionist. There is, perhaps understandably, an ignorance in the wider country about Pittsburgh's history, even though the city's story is intrinsic to the national narrative—the latter isn't comprehensible without the former—and the past weighs heavily here. "A city with heft—that's how a friend who moved here...described it," writes retired *Pittsburgh Post-Gazette* columnist Brian O'Neill in his collection entitled, yes, *The Paris of Appalachia: Pittsburgh in the Twenty-First Century.* "Victorian wealth remains evident in our architecture, our culture, our foundations, our hospitals and our universities." O'Neill explains that the Gilded Age sheen still visible under the rust on our belts is intrinsic to the aesthetic of the city and reflective of its story of rise, decline and perhaps resurrection.

American capitalism was built on Pittsburgh steel, iron, coke, copper, glass and aluminum; robber barons like Carnegie, Frick, Westinghouse, Heinz and the Mellons were the veritable kings of American ascent, but their power was filched through the exploitation of (frequently immigrant) labor. Contradictions define Pittsburgh—it's the metropolis whose rivers were lined with belching steel mills but that also hosted the world's first major modern art exhibition, the second-largest city in a commonwealth founded as a utopia but that eventually contributed to our current ecological precipice. This is a region that has yet to fully acknowledge that its greatest cultural contributions of music and literature were made by its Black citizens and that it's long been home to a radical political tradition too often obscured by the illustrious names of the powerful chiseled on our buildings. Even more shocking is that this city renowned for grime and filth, soot and smog, is almost incandescently and irresistibly beautiful, what the poet Jack Gilbert described as a "tough heaven." In my first book about the city, *An Alternative History of Pittsburgh*, I write that this place is "large and multitudinous, multifaceted, multifractured; it is complex, contradictory, and confusing." Neither that book nor this one was written as rejoinder to the man-child—he's too irrelevant to deserve that—nor were they written to actually *be* a history, counterintuitive as that sounds. Besides, there are already excellent historiographical accounts—Franklin Toker's *Pittsburgh: A New Portrait*, Martin Aurand's *The Spectator and the Topographical City* and the magisterial forerunner of them all, Stefan Laurent's half-century-old *Pittsburgh: The Story of an American City* (illustrated with stunning photographs by W. Eugene Smith). Readers who consult them will get a brilliant grounding in the facts, but what I wanted to do—and still want to do—is assemble "a diary, a dream journal, a wooden shelf packed with interesting rocks and shells." Such an endeavor was never undertaken by me as a brief or an apology, or as conventional scholarship, but rather to keep the paradoxes of Pittsburgh in view.

More fundamentally, it must be remembered how Pittsburgh's terrain was responsible for its explosive success, and the city has maintained it even through decline. "Geography is destiny," Toker writes in *Pittsburgh: A New Portrait*. "For a hundred years Pittsburgh extracted the land's resources, grinding up sandstone to make glass, mining coal for making steel, and refining oil at the very beginning of a global industry." But as concerns Pittsburgh, there is also something intangible and ineffable about that terrain, what the ancient Romans called genius loci, the individual spirit of place. There is a reason why longtime locals are excited to take newcomers through the Fort Pitt Tunnel: how the individual perspective transmutes from the humdrum scrabble of the highway into an exit of brilliant, bursting luminescence, skyscrapers arrayed beneath you along the rivers, with the sweep of hills on either side, homes clinging to their incline like adobes in a canyon. To the east, Oakland is arrayed in long blocks of low neoclassical buildings covered in gleaming limestone, appearing like the Acropolis but with the whole neighborhood punctuated by the University of Pittsburgh's Cathedral of Learning, an absurd and sublime neo-Gothic skyscraper. There are communities like Polish Hill, rowhouses on the narrow and crooked streets slinking their way toward the green-patina dome of the Immaculate Heart of Mary (an imitation in miniature of St. Peter's Basilica) or Squirrel Hill with its verdant slope nestled between the wilderness of Frick and Schenley Parks, situated at the axes of Forbes and Murray, lined with Chinese restaurants, kosher grocery stores, synagogues and bookstores. As the *New Yorker's* architecture critic Brendan Gill unironically wrote in 1989, "The three most beautiful cities in the world are Paris; St. Petersburg, Russia; and Pittsburgh. If Pittsburgh were situated somewhere in the heart of Europe, tourists would eagerly journey hundreds of miles out of their way to visit it."

In all of its glory and filth, through the triumph and oppression, Pittsburgh is a metonymy for this nation and for its own conflicted history. Today, factories are turned into luxury condominiums and shopping centers placed atop repurposed slag heaps. It reminds me of the observation of Montaigne's secretary on their visit to similarly hilly Rome in 1580, where "in certain places we were walking over the roof-ridges of houses still intact….We walked on the tops of the old walls, which the rains and the coach wheels occasionally bring into sight." Instead of the Colosseum, we have the Carrie Blast Furnace; rather than the Pantheon, there are the Homestead Steel Works' smokestacks. But just as Rome's monuments signified the ideology that sustained their empire, for better and frequently worse, so too are the ruins of Pittsburgh representative of our own empire's fortunes. O'Neill writes in *The Paris of Appalachia* that "most American cities have yet to see their finest architecture, their highest population, their greatest impact on the world. We almost certainly have. We used to be a much bigger deal, and then we stopped being one." If there was one argument I ventured in my previous book, or conclusion rendered, or maybe just gimmick proffered, it was that to write a history of Pittsburgh is to write a history of America. The book you are now holding has both less and more grandiose aims. If the first book focused on history, on that process of ordering one damn thing after another, then this current volume is more concerned with what it feels like to be a Pittsburgher today, with what our identity could be configured as. In that regard, this is a much more self-consciously personal book. If I used to argue that writing a history of Pittsburgh was as if writing a history of America, now I'm maybe content to admit that it's more like writing an autobiography.

Aforementioned East Liberty poet Jack Gilbert spent his life in New York, the Greek isles, Tokyo and San Francisco, but he would imagine Pittsburgh often. In one lyric, Gilbert recounts taking care of the baby of his Danish girlfriend. He writes of "changing him and making him laugh. / I would say *Pittsburgh* softly each time before throwing him up. Whisper *Pittsburgh* with / my mouth against the tiny ear and throw him higher." Gilbert's narrator knows that his relationship has an expiration date and that these brief, happy moments with her infant will not last. Yet he wishes to leave a bit of himself, a bit of where he has come from, "even the smallest trace," with the child. "So that all his life her son would feel gladness / unaccountably when anyone spoke of the ruined / city of steel in America. Each time almost / remembering something maybe important that got lost."

Now, let me whisper, *Pittsburgh*.

Chapter 1

THEORY AND PRACTICE
OF THE YINZER

The city center of Glasgow, Scotland—that iron-and-glass-forged, cobblestoned fortress of a hilly, rainy, foggy metropolis—is bisected by the dueling high streets of Buchanan and Sauchiehall. There are any number of landmarks to draw your attention if ambling down either of these bustling thoroughfares as the last squibs of Caledonian light fight their losing battle of attrition during a brisk November afternoon. For six months in 2006, Glasgow was my home across the Atlantic, and I often spent those glum Scottish afternoons in precisely this sort of aimless wandering, past the Victorian magnificence of the exposed-girder Queen Street rail station and the imposing, imperial grandeur of St. George's Square; the smooth, modernist sandstone edifice of the Glasgow Royal Concert Hall with its green-patina statue of the slightly depressed-looking Scottish first minister Donald Dewar and the Palladian, neoclassical granite of the Gallery of Modern Art with its equestrian statue of the Duke of Wellington in front, inevitably vandalized again each night in the exact same way, with some waggish Glaswegian placing an orange traffic cone upon that esteemed head.

Glasgow, that city of some six hundred thousand people on the River Clyde, once Great Britain's veritable second city, despite its reputation for filth and grime grew rich in the nineteenth century on coal mining and iron forging, textiles and food canning and most of all shipbuilding but saw a precipitous decline in both esteem and population with the disastrous neoliberal economic reforms of a generation ago. As a Pittsburgher, this was a narrative I already knew. Because it has always been a place strung between capital and labor, the wealthy and the workers, Glasgow long ago developed a widespread, irreverent radicalism, as evidenced by the conical crown atop the fussy English Duke of Wellington—a perspective about injustice and absurdity that wasn't unfamiliar to me either. Listening to punk at that incomparable dive King Tut's Wah Wah Hut or enjoying an Irish ceilidh at Failte Pub, pounding a pint of Guinness at Waxy O'Connor's or Tennant's at the Old Toll, getting a curry from Karahi Palace or a late-night doner at the appropriately named Best Kebab, grabbing an Irn-Bru to cure a hangover at Boots the Chemist or devouring a Cornish pasty purchased from Greg's—it all felt strangely similar even if so obviously different, as if looking at your own reflection through a slightly opaque bubble-glass window at any one of the pubs lining Buchanan and Sauchiehall. *Glasgow*, I thought, *is kind of like Pittsburgh*. And then, walking through Glasgow again, I hear it: "There was a couple other of yins as well." *What?*

First, a confession—I never heard that exact sentence, though I heard many similar ones with that particular second-person plural in evidence. This example is from the Scottish author James Kelman's 1994 controversial stream-of-consciousness, Booker Prize—winning, working-class classic "grit lit" novel *How Late It Was, How Late*, penned in often indecipherable phonetic Glaswegian. Incidentally, variations on the word *yin* or *yins* appear sixty-seven

The Glasgow docks along the River Clyde, 1860. *Wikimedia Commons, distributed under a CC-BY 2.0 license.*

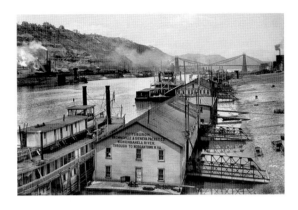

The Monongahela Wharf, 1904.
*Wikimedia Commons, distributed
under a CC-BY 2.0 license.*

times in Kelman's novel, a tough, bruising, obscene and profane account of a shoplifting, alcoholic ex-con navigating the absurdities of Scotland's largest city. Despite the anger from many among the English literati at this first Scottish book to win a Booker, *How Late It Was, How Late* is written in the sort of dialect that can only really be heard by people from "Used to Be Important" places, from the cauldrons of industry and the forges of labor, from the cities that built the world but were then abandoned when factories closed and mills shuttered, only to have to reinvent themselves over and over. "Folk take a battering but, they do; they get born and they get brought up and they get fuckt," writes Kelman. "That's the story; the cot to the fucking funeral pyre." There is more than a spiritual congruence between Glasgow and Pittsburgh, as Kelman's "yins" would indicate, the *s* that ends that word so perilously close a sibilant to the *z* in *yinz* and the words so nearly used identically. For those unfamiliar with *yinz*—though I imagine if you're currently reading this book, you most likely know what it means, albeit it's becoming increasingly rare in usage—it's simply the Western Pennsylvania second-person plural, the Pittsburgh equivalent of *y'all* down South or *youse* in Jersey and New York.

It is, admittedly to many outside the region (and to some within it), a strange-sounding word. Where there is a certain sense in how *you* and *all* can be smoosh-mouthed over time into that aouthern all-purpose word, *yinz* has a slightly alien quality about it, a combination of sounds that don't quite make sense, a shibboleth of identity to those who live in Pittsburgh and, apparently, Glasgow. Because Kelman's "yins" and the "yinz" you hear at Ritter's Diner in Bloomfield, Gough's Tavern in Greenfield, Gene's Place in South Oakland or the Squirrel Hill Café literally have the same origin. As any good Glaswegian would tell you, *yin* simply means "one," but though obscure, it's actually the same with Pittsburgh's most distinctive linguistic attribute. Just as *y'all* is a compression of two other words, so does *yinz* come from *you ones*. That phrase is a direct translation of the Gallic Scots, where the second-person plural is perfectly grammatically correct. Calling it the "most salient morphosyntactic feature of local speech," Carnegie Mellon University rhetoric professor Barbara Johnson explains in her study *Speaking Pittsburghese: The Story of a Dialect* (published as part of the prestigious Oxford Studies in Sociolinguistics series) that "'yinz' was brought to America by Scotch-Irish immigrants…the descendants of Protestant people from Scotland and northern England." From the shores of the Clyde then to the Monongahela, Allegheny and Ohio, it seems that my ears on Sauchiehall and Buchanan weren't in error.

Because I've occasionally fooled myself into pretending that education can easily obscure markers of regional identity and class, I never hear my own Pittsburgh accent when I'm actually in the city, and by no means would mine sound particularly thick to any born Yinzer. Yet when I'm somewhere else, particularly in the Acela Corridor of the Northeast, I apparently sound like I'm sitting on a frayed red canvas stool at Chandos in Homestead drinking an Iron City (note that the first word is pronounced exactly like the prefix in *Irn-Bru*, the Scottish pop I mentioned earlier). I've never uttered *yinz* in any way other than ironically, but if vocabulary can be a choice, pronunciation is destiny. To wit, words like *cot* and *caught* sound identical when I speak them—a characteristic of Pittsburgh English; when tired, I pronounce the "vowel in words that rhyme without as a monophthong rather than a diphthong" as Johnson writes, which is to say that *down* becomes "dahn," *town* becomes "tahn," *field* becomes "filled," *steel* becomes "still," and so on. Other markers are sprinkled in as well; I've got the tendency to convert declarative sentences into what sounds like an interrogative, and dropping the words *to be* from a sentence (as in "The car needs washed") sounds completely grammatically correct to me, even though I have a PhD in English. Finally, there is the telltale vocabulary, the more conscious aspects of dialect that in Pittsburgh can include everything from calling a vacuum cleaner a sweeper to saying that a nosy person is being nebby, telling people that a room that needs to be cleaned has to be red-up or describing a disagreeable person as a jagoff.

The latter is supposedly from the burr-like thorns of the English and Scottish Midlands jagger-bush, but everybody in Pittsburgh knows that the insult is just as obscene as it sounds and references exactly what you think it does, even if until 2016 it could still be published sans censor marks in the *Pittsburgh Post-Gazette*. This is the lexicography of a thousand black-and-gold novelty T-shirts sold from sidewalk stalls on Saturdays in

Smallman Street in the gritty Strip District, circa 2007, a neighborhood that sells a thousand permutations of Yinz-ware in its numerous stalls and stores. *Wikimedia Commons, distributed under a CC-BY 2.0 license.*

the Strip District or proudly worn at a Steelers tailgate. "To outsiders, the Pittsburgh dialect may sound odd," notes Andy Masich, director of the Senator John Heinz III Regional History Museum in his foreword to *Pittsburghese: From Ahrn to Yinz.* "Even Pittsburghers argue whether jagoff can be uttered in polite society." Because there are few famous examples of a Pittsburgh dialect—Michael Keaton speaks with a wonderful accent, especially as the character Beetlejuice, and outsider Nick Kroll does a fairly good imitation in the skit "Pawnsylvania" from his national sketch comedy show—it tends to confuse people. When entering a hardware store in the small Massachusetts town that I lived in for two years, there was simply incredulity and incomprehension at how I was speaking (though perhaps that was just Boston friendliness). They had none of the *r*'s, and I had all of them. They thought that I was a pirate.

As an accent, Pittsburgh English may be centered in the city, but today it's more likely to be heard in the outer counties of Western Pennsylvania. Linguistically it's clearly a variation on northern Appalachian English; *yinz* or some permutation is frequently heard in western Maryland, eastern Ohio and the West Virginia panhandle. Within Pittsburgh, the accent has a curious aspect to it: that vaguely twangy Appalachian pronunciation with all those loan words from Polish, Neapolitan and Yiddish, making the dialect sound a bit like if somebody from Brooklyn was doing a really poor imitation of somebody from Kentucky, an urban *Deadwood* kind of talk. Pittsburghese, Western Pennsylvania English or, technically, the North American North

Midland dialect—however you choose to identify the accent, what's unassailable is that such a way of speaking is strongly identified with the archetypal figure of the Yinzer. As a Townie or a Southie is to Boston, so is the Yinzer to Pittsburgh. Inextricably bound with issues of class and race, a Yinzer embodies the stereotypes associated with White blue-collar Pittsburghers. If someone's voice evidences that "vowel in words that rhyme without as a monophthong rather than a diphthong" as Johnson put it, then certain assumptions are made.

In popular culture, rightly or wrongly, a Yinzer is understood as somebody for whom nostalgia is a birthright (often focused around 1974, when the Steelers first won the Super Bowl). Their wardrobe consists of only black and gold; the needle on their car's radio never wavers from 96.9, the home for classic rock; and the men sport goatees or beards, maybe a mullet (true for the women as well). If responsible for shoveling the filthy, black, exhaust-stained snow to make a parking spot on a narrow cobblestoned street in front of their rowhouse in the depths of February, a Yinzer will most definitely mark their territory with a flimsy folding chair that best not be moved by an interloper. A Yinzer subsists on a diet of kielbasa and pierogis, salads and sandwiches heaped high with French fries and draft after draft of Iron City Beer (maybe Rolling Rock). In the stereotype, and perhaps the reality, Yinzers manifest a strange fusion of friendliness and toughness, an erratic personality that can seemingly swing between Brooklyn crankiness and Peoria pleasant, an extroverted, gregarious people whose conversation can sound like screaming. Yinzers are kitsch made manifest. More than anything, in a metropolitan area that finally sees its population growing again after decades of decline, a Yinzer is somebody whose roots have been here for generations.

Like any broad portrait, there are things recognizable in such descriptions and there are things that are cartoonish. Certainly, a generation or two ago—when the word *yinz* was heard far more frequently—the self-designation *Yinzer* would have been anathema. Now, however, there is an entire cottage industry of Yinzerhood, from the (excellent) T-shirts at Commonwealth Print Shop to the Yinz Coffee chain. Stereotypes about Pittsburgh are celebrated on hats, beer koozies, coasters, mugs, scarves, jackets and a truly horrifying doll called the Debbie Yappin' Yinzer Talking Plush. Despite the preponderance of genuine Pittsburgh accents, from the much-missed and now departed Steelers radio broadcaster Myron "Yoi and Double Yoi" Cope to the beloved 1980s rock musician Donnie "Dahnnie" Iris, the current most famous Yinzer is Greensburg native Curt Wootton of the contemporary web series *Pittsburgh Dad*. Premiering in 2011 and quickly gaining viral popularity throughout the metropolitan region, *Pittsburgh Dad* is a sort of meta-comedy deconstruction of the sitcom, featuring only Wootton facing the camera, often in a stereotypical "Pittsburgh Room" (a sort of faux wood–lined basement man cave filled with sports paraphernalia) speaking in an exaggerated accent and namechecking any number of references from Eat 'n Park to Giant Eagle to Kennywood, with his monologue punctuated by an almost mocking laugh track. Wearing a pair of what can only be described as fantastically unhip glasses and a polo shirt with the IBEW Local logo, Pittsburgh Dad is often drunk, frequently screaming at his children, a superstitious if poorly catechized Catholic and disturbingly obsessed with the Steelers and Penguins. Total views of *Pittsburgh Dad*'s videos are at an astounding seventy-seven million.

Like a lot of Yinzer humor, there is a spirit of affection when the *Pittsburgh Dad* videos are shared among locals. With Yinzer jokes more generally, however, there is the threat that loving caricature can veer into some sort of working-class minstrel show, not to mention when Yinzer-hood becomes a means of separating out "Real Pittsburghers," a way of excluding recent transplants or minorities whose roots in the region can go back just as far as those of anyone with the accent (there is, notably, a seeming contradiction in the idea of there being Black Yinzers). That's not to say that *Pittsburgh Dad* isn't funny—it often is, though I imagine the humor doesn't translate well to those who aren't already in on the jokes. More importantly, it's not to say that *Pittsburgh Dad* doesn't have a bit of subversive bite to it as well—it does. A particularly funny episode contrasts Pittsburgh's burgeoning reputation as a weird hipster Mecca in the mold of Portland with the folksy provincialism of the past when Wootton accidentally takes his children to Anthrocon, the annual convention of the plush animal–dressed fetishists known as furries, having perilously and accidentally assumed that it was a gathering of sports mascots. *Pittsburgh Dad* deftly interlaces the warm and the cynical with an almost Glaswegian proficiency, as when Wootton recounts the mythic tale of the suburban Century III Mall's genesis, claiming that the "steel mills would transport their toxic waste by train to a little slice of heaven in West Mifflin called Brown's Dump.…Then they'd slowly spill out that glowing, molten toxic waste onto the hillside, into the environment, and it was no big deal.…In a few months, up sprouted the best one million square foot of commerce the Western world had ever seen!" Delivered in the accent or not—maybe especially because it is—the monologue has a bit more fang than might

The Midlothian hills in Scotland between Glasgow and Edinburgh, 2010. *Photograph by Richard Webb, distributed under a CC-BY 2.0 license.*

The Allegheny Mountains near Blue Knob, Pennsylvania, 2007. Both the Scottish mountains and the Appalachians are geologically the same mountain range. *Photograph by Joe Calzarette, distributed under a CC-BY 2.0 license.*

first be assumed. *Pittsburgh Dad* isn't exactly *How Late It Was, How Late*, but it's not entirely perpendicular to it either.

There's a reason for the popularity of *Pittsburgh Dad*, as well as, more broadly, the niche of Yinzer branding. Australian urban theorist Laura Crommelin writes in the journal *Place Branding and Public Diplomacy* that such representations of "yinzer culture…function as both DIY urban branding and as a reflection of local reactions to Pittsburgh's economic, social and brand transition." Of all the major metropolitan regions to be cratered out by the neoliberal industrial collapse of the late 1980s—Cleveland, Detroit, Flint—Pittsburgh has by far had the most successful resurgence, bolstered by the tremendous Gilded Age wealth that still powered deep-pocketed nonprofit foundations within the city, as well as the transition to a medical- and technology-based economy. In such a context, the proud embrace of Yinzerdom is a type of resistance against new economic forces that threaten to transform the region, the same sorts of economic forces that every native Pittsburgher knows once demolished it. *Yinz* has moved from the realm of actual conversation and into the hipster domain of ironic reclamation, of screen printed T-shirts with Pittsburgh lingo on them or handmade cross-stitches that say things like "Red Up Dis Room," "J'eet Yet?," n'at, though as Johnson said in an interview with the *Pittsburgh City Paper*'s Chris Potter, "People can do this lovingly, and I think a lot of the hipster stuff is kind of loving."

Like any nostalgia kick, there are dangers to such representations, though. Yinzer discourse can solidify a genuine division, especially between those of us who have been here forever and those just now discovering the beauty of Pittsburgh. It can confirm the suspicions about the city being backward, provincial and insular. Even more insidiously, there is a way in which it bolsters some truly noxious understandings of who belongs and who doesn't. You'll note that while a Yinzer can be many things—Scots-Irish and Carpatho-Rusyn, Czech and Slovak, Greek and Italian, Polish and Ukrainian, German and Irish Catholic—hardly ever is the Yinzer envisioned as Black (or Asian, or Hispanic). As Damon Young accurately half-jokes in his book *What Doesn't Kill You Makes You Blacker: A Memoir in Essays*, "Pittsburgh itself is so segregated that any place within a ten-mile radius of the city with more than seven black people there at one time feels like the Essence Festival." Then there are the complexities surrounding the self-designation of the term *Yinzer*: the way in which, despite how affectionately such portrayals may be intended, there is still something a bit insulting about the whole thing.

When I was speaking about my previous book on the city, *An Alternative History of Pittsburgh*, I was at a loss following one audience member's question about what my intent had been in writing the title. Fumbling through various inchoate justifications for why I'd written it, explaining how my goal had been to express an aspect of the city that was complicated, nuanced, sophisticated and not always adoringly positive, I may have said that I wanted to "avoid writing a particular type of book." The woman who'd asked the question clarified my meaning: "A Yinzer book?" That was exactly it—I didn't want to write a Yinzer book. I wanted to give a sense of my love for Pittsburgh while avoiding halcyon and corny expressions of mindless civic boosterism; it was my intent to try and express a bit of the grit and determination of the city, but I was loathe to have anything too Yinzer-y about the whole thing (that particular second-person plural appears only once in the entire book).

Why the chagrin? Why my own Pittsburgh cringe? "Sometimes we're so afraid of what others think, we're afraid to declare who we are," writes former *Pittsburgh Post-Gazette* columnist Brian O'Neill in his seminal collection *The Paris of Appalachia: Pittsburgh in the Twenty-First Century*. "It's not East Coast. It's just Pittsburgh, and there's no place like it. That's both its blessing and its curse." O'Neill's book went a long way toward popularizing that particular nickname, which I've also always been ambivalent about. From a geographic perspective, the placement of Pittsburgh in that mythologized mountain range is unassailable. Allegheny County is unequivocally the most populous in the entirety of the Appalachians. Yet the connotations of "Appalachian" are what they are, so that I—along with many people in the region—have historically avoided it. A bit like the accent, there's a sense in which the associations reflect something derogatory about how others see us rather than a reality that we know to be true. And yet, despite its complexities, despite what's admittedly problematic about it, why avoid speaking in the dialect, why obscure the Pittsburgh in our own voice?

The accent hasn't endeared us to many. In 2014, Pittsburgh beat out my wife's native Rhode Island in a Gawker magazine sweet sixteen–style competition to find the nation's ugliest accent, much to the delight of local news media, for the city's honor would have been besmirched had it been decided that ours was only the second-worst accent in the United States. To be sure, there is a cankered kind of pride at such national scorn, an estimably admirable combination of confidence and humility that knows precisely what such rejections and mockery are worth. There is something also kind of incredible in the circuitous route by which *yinz* became so intrinsic to the Pittsburgh identity, this linguistic coelacanth hidden on the

Pittsburgh skyline from Mount Washington, autumn of 2022. *Photograph by Cbail19, distributed under a CC-BY 2.0 license.*

hills and in the valleys of Western Pennsylvania. From Ulster and Derry, Birmingham and Manchester, Edinburgh and Scotland, *yinz* was carried into the frontiers of Western Pennsylvania, now spoken by those who've never seen Midlothian or the Clyde—now it is rather the grandchildren of Krakow and Warsaw, Hamburg and Frankfurt, Dublin and Kerry, Prague and Budapest, Charleston and Richmond, Naples and Pescara who speak this venerable Scottish word. Few of us are directly descended from the Caledonian hills anymore, but like any example of glorious hybridized culture, we took some of that language and mixed it with a million different things. It's true that there can be a sense in which the barrier to entry is high in Pittsburgh, but I've often joked that membership can be more affordable than you might expect, for if you like us and you're willing to wear black and gold, you're given a ticket.

There was an exceedingly friendly gentleman whom I knew from the Pacific Northwest who moved here and full-throatedly embraced the poetic necessity of the word *yinz*, that great gender-neutral pronoun. Despite not being the fourth generation to live in his family's house in Greenfield or Brookline, there was something of the spiritual Yinzer about him. All of which reminds me of a strange and beautiful column published in 1914 by

James G. Connell Jr., an executive at the West Penn Paper Company of all things, that was titled "The Pittsburgh Creed." Connell wrote, "I believe in Pittsburgh the powerful—the progressive....I believe in Pittsburgh of the present, and her people—possessing the virtue of all nations—fused through the melting pot to a greater potency for good....I believe that those who know Pittsburgh love her, 'her rocks and rills, and templed hills.' I believe that Pittsburgh's mighty forces are reproduced in a mighty people, stanch like the hills,—true like steel." Nothing is backward, provincial or insular about that. And I think of all of us, this diversity of peoples, maybe first from Scotland and England but joined by immigrants from Germany and Ireland, Italy and Poland, Black Americans coming north from Dixie and Jews fleeing eastern European pogroms and now arrivals from China and India, Ethiopia and Nepal, and the glorious strangeness and beauty and absurdity that we can all make this culture of Pittsburgh our own, and change it a bit, and make it better. What shame is there in being a Yinzer, whence the "Pittsburgh Creed" was derived? When Kelman won the Booker Prize in 1994, the British press was outraged that a book written in what was such a supposedly low dialect was given those laurels, offended that the author had the audacity to hear anything beautiful in Glaswegian. He answered such objections in his acceptance speech, saying, "[My] culture and my language have the right to exist, and no one has the authority to dismiss that." What do yinz think of that?

Chapter 2

NINETY NEIGHBORHOODS

y favorite neighborhood technically doesn't exist. For a mile and a half,
stretching from North Oakland to East Liberty, Baum Boulevard and
Centre Avenue run parallel to each other in what's for Pittsburgh a brief
rectilinear grid made possible by the several bridges above the Allegheny River
Valley, domain of the busway, freight rail and Amtrack. The neighborhood is
an assortment of medical laboratories, high-rise residences, old warehouses
(many now loft apartments), former factories, elegant churches, massive
grocery stores and various and sundry businesses from dry cleaners to diners,
all of it punctuated by the massive turquoise-colored and glass-paned dome
of Motor Square Garden, built during the Gilded Age as a car dealership for
Pittsburgh steel barons and variously a venue for concerts and boxing prize
fights and, briefly, a failed high-end shopping mall in the 1980s, now going to
waste as the world's most elegant AAA office. Few Pittsburghers would name
this twenty-seven blocks as their favorite neighborhood—perhaps they are
immune to the charm of aging car dealerships and autobody shops, chain
restaurants and funeral homes—but this area always had a noirish romance
for me, the experience of an unmistakably urban environment, with grit
and beauty comingling: driving down Baum or Centre, asphalt slick with
rain puddles reflecting the red neon from the sign at Jimmy Tsang's Chinese
Restaurant (now sadly closed) or examining the intricate rococo masonry of
the stalwart prewar high-rises over the small triangle of green that is Morrow
Park, all of it soundtracked by Miles Davis's *Kind of Blue* or Tom Waits's *The
Heart of Saturday Night*. None of this is actually a neighborhood, however,
according to the City of Pittsburgh; it's in fact composed of leftover parts

The turquoise-colored dome of Motor Square Garden, built in 1898. *Photograph by Father Pitt, distributed under a CC1.0 license.*

of five other neighborhoods—Oakland, Shadyside, Bloomfield, Friendship and East Liberty.

Pittsburgh neighborhoods are both distinctive and indeterminate, which generates geographic debates among residents that are almost Talmudic. Nobody would confuse those five neighborhoods—tweedy, regal and academic Oakland with its massive limestone university buildings and its bronze monuments; bourgeoise Shadyside with its boutiques, cafés, Tudor mansions, Georgian townhomes and Cape Anne houses; working-class Italian Bloomfield's long line of rowhouses decorated with statues of the Virgin Mary and St. Francis; bohemian Friendship's subdivided Victorian mansions composed of red brick and heavy dark wood, decorated interiors of red and yellow and blue stained glass; and now bustling East Liberty, which after decades of urban blight is suddenly defined by the scaffolding and cranes constructing new high-rises. Because the corridor between Baum and Centre is so different from those other neighborhoods—*so clearly its own thing*—this fictional area is like an easement between those communities, an alleyway running between apartment buildings or maybe the shared backyards of parallel rowhouses. Baum and Centre function as a zipper suturing together these constituent places, containing a bit of the essence of each of those neighborhoods while remaining its own dogged thing. Once, the City Fathers attempted to rectify this; briefly, in 2006, the administration of Mayor Bob O'Conner announced that this corridor would be defined as Pittsburgh's ninety-first neighborhood, though it was given the rather indecorous name Baum-Centre, which in our accent sounds like Bomb Center. I've always been partial to naming it Morrow Park after its single patch of green. Regardless, the designation never took, and it remains what it is: the cast-off back portions of five other neighborhoods that border one another. Despite that, for the four years that I lived on Centre Avenue, I still considered myself to be a proud citizen of this unnamed place, which I shall forever call the Limbo District.

"The secret to Pittsburgh's strength lies in its neighborhoods," writes architectural historian Franklin Toker in *Pittsburgh: A New Portrait*. "The neighborhoods kept Pittsburgh afloat through the collapse of the steel industry and the decades of economic uncertainty that followed, and it is their continuing strength that makes Pittsburgh unsinkable." For sure, every municipality has individual neighborhoods, or at least most do, and yet the ninety individual communities of Pittsburgh are, when taken in their totality, more than the whole of Pittsburgh itself. Primarily the result of Pittsburgh's fractured landscape, bisected by rivers, valleys and hills, these neighborhoods are defined by geography and terrain, topography and ethnicity. Troy Hill, Squirrel Hill, Polish Hill and the Hill District—Pittsburgh announces the landscape in the names themselves; from Mount Washington to the Southside Flats, this is a city where settlements were not decided by ruler

The massive steeple of East Liberty Presbyterian Church as seen from Baum Boulevard. *Wikimedia Commons, distributed under a CC-BY 2.0 license.*

and compass but by landscape as laid down by God Himself (though some ponds may have been filled in and some hills moved along the way).

Josette Fitzgibbons, the Urban Redevelopment Authority neighborhood district manager, was quoted in an article from 2018 by Katie Blackley for WESA saying that the local government's goal was "to say, 'We are a city, but we have 90 neighborhoods and each one has its own character and these are the things that are great about each of these neighborhoods.'" There's a bit of marketing to all of this, and neighborhood divisions can be inexact—as evidenced by all the unofficial "internal" neighborhoods—but it would be an error to interpret this as boilerplate. Pittsburgh's neighborhoods are shockingly diverse, an assemblage of ninety often radically different communities that all somehow share the same city. Like one of those tropical archipelagos studied by nineteenth-century naturalists wherein a stunning array of creatures zoological and botanical could evolve on discrete islands, Pittsburgh neighborhoods frequently host their own singular ecosystems, so that nobody would be able to mistake Highland Park for Hazelwood, Morningside for Manchester, Point Breeze for Perry Hilltop, Ridgemont for Regent Square. A beneficial preponderance for the city's growing film industry, for if you need Chicago's Hyde Park, you go to Shadyside; if you want Boston's Southie, you can film in Greenfield; South Philly is in Bloomfield; Crown Heights is in South Squirrel Hill; North Squirrel Hill is Brookline, Massachusetts; and Manhattan is just Downtown, though of course all of those places are really just pure Pittsburgh.

Such kaleidoscopic multiplicity is conveyed by Ron Donoughe, who painted an evocative, fascinating and, most of all, beautiful series of ninety paintings representing each one of the officially recognized neighborhoods. First exhibited in the spacious former galleries of the Pittsburgh Center for the Arts in 2015, when that museum was housed inside Mellon Park's yellow Scaife Building, as elegant as a wedding cake, Donoughe's cycle of paintings captures the city's visual landscape, the way in which a thousand different hilly vantage points lend themselves to a seeming limitless panoply of views and panoramas, vistas and perspective. Donoughe is a plein air painter who creates in the open air. The Pittsburgh series was rendered over twelve months, and the manner in which the artist represented each community can be particular, personal and poetic. Evocative of Edward Hopper in how masterfully he is able to convey both the bliss and loneliness of urban life, Donoughe eschews the obvious in favor of the granular and the idiosyncratic. For example, in his composition *Central Oakland*, Donoughe doesn't re-create the Gothic skyscraper of the University of Pittsburgh's

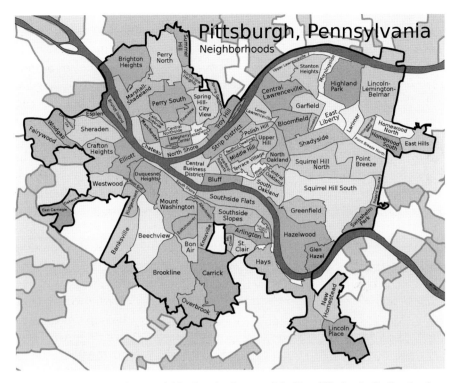

A map of Pittsburgh's ninety neighborhoods. *Courtesy of the City of Pittsburgh, distributed under a CC-BY 2.0 license.*

iconic Cathedral of Learning (though it's featured in several paintings from neighboring communities where the tower is visible), but rather, he focuses only on the red-painted and iron cross-hatched doors of Heinz Chapel, an exact replica of Paris's thirteenth-century Sainte-Chappelle. It's the sort of detail that's more in keeping with a person's daily perambulations, the little things that somebody on their commute maybe focuses on for a minute or so before they're on their way—the way in which a true New Yorker might pay more attention to the hot dog vendor in front of the Empire State Building than to the skyscraper.

The series presents a Pittsburgh that is like a gem that refracts light in an endless number of ways every time you turn it. Clearly indebted to the eighteenth-century Japanese watercolorist Katsushika Hokusai's iconic *Thirty-Six Views of Mount Fuji*, with its understanding of the infinite potential implicit in an individual location, Donoughe's series gestures toward the magnificent array of possibility. In *South Oakland*, he depicts a red-trimmed Victorian on the Boulevard of the Allies, shabby and blighted, a fire escape snaking up toward

the second story in a residence that's clearly been divided into apartments, the lot next to it vacant, perhaps where another home has been demolished. *East Liberty* uses the Gothic detailing of that neighborhood's dominant Presbyterian cathedral to frame brilliant local sculptor Virgil Cantini's 1969 *Joy of Life*, a modernist iron fountain with an assortment of abstracted figurines dancing in a circle. By contrast to such urban cosmopolitanism, *Perry South* shows two working-class detached single-family homes, a green-paneled one and a white-paneled one, at the end of a wooded cul-de-sac that looks more rural than metropolitan. Meanwhile, *Polish Hill* presents the massive green-patina dome of Immaculate Heart of Mary Church—an exact replica of St. Peter's Basilica, albeit at a fraction of the scale—looming over the modest rowhouses clinging to the scrubby mountainside. *Squirrel Hill North* shows a large, comfortable Craftsman-style house on Beechwood Boulevard with a sloping red terra-cotta roof, while *Squirrel Hill South* ignores the rowhouses and apartment buildings that characterize that neighborhood in favor of a pastoral scene in Schenley Park, the towers of Downtown visible on the horizon. Similarly, in *Upper Lawrenceville*, Donoughe conjures all of the dense, tightly packed homes of the concrete and cobblestoned formerly working-class neighborhood, the skyscrapers of Downtown erupting skyward only a mile or so in the distance.

Opposite: The skyline of Oakland as seen from the South Side. *Photograph by Tylert220, distributed under a CC-BY 2.0 license.*

Above: The iconic red doors to Heinz Chapel. *Photograph by Tim Engelman, distributed under a CC-BY 2.0 license.*

East Liberty. Courtesy of Ron Donoughe and the Senator John Heinz III Regional Pittsburgh History Center.

Collected in the book *Pittsburgh: 90 Neighborhoods*, the series presents a panoply of Pittsburgh fragments, a view of the city filtered through separate moments, brief interplays of light and shadow on brick and stone, concrete and glass, iron and steel. There is no "Grand Theory of Pittsburgh" formulated by Donoughe, for that would be impossible, but there are certain thematic resonances that reoccur: the working-class brick rowhouses with their concrete stoops; the nineteenth-century stone mansions; the way homes slither up preposterously steep inclines, where they are dominated by the smokestacks of forlorn steel mills; and the strange interplay of nature and industry, the manner in which scrub and kudzu can fill the gulfs, gullies and gorges that separate neighborhoods, the hills and hollows, the rivers and embankments. "Pittsburgh neighbors have a special, spiritual attachment to the city—especially people who grew up here—that you don't always find in other towns," writes Taylor Fowler in an appreciation for the website Very Local. "Generations upon generations live on the same block, pass down homes, and have Pittsburgh become part of them." Which is not to say that geography alone is destiny, but there are any number of arbitrary divisions

Ron Donoughe's *Polish Hill Morning. Courtesy of Ron Donoughe and the Senator John Heinz III Regional Pittsburgh History Center.*

made by ruler, the rhizomatic network of streets in the wedge-shaped map of Pittsburgh as constrained by the three rivers generating boundaries, hence where debates often emerge. For example, Squirrel Hill, which is Pittsburgh's most populous neighborhood at around twenty-six thousand people, is actually any number of smaller communities across a range of socioeconomic statuses, though no boundary is more certain than that of Forbes Avenue, dividing the area into north and south regions officially recognized by city government. South Squirrel Hill is often cobblestoned and steep, homes crowding together toward the Beth Sholom synagogue, which looms over the community like a golem in repose, while tree-lined North Squirrel Hill is an abode of Craftsman homes and Tudors. According to a rumor, when Pittsburgh's beloved Jewish grandmother Sophie Masloff was elected mayor in 1988, the high school–educated former child worker in a Hill District cigar factory officially moved the boundary between the two neighborhoods ever so slightly so that a sliver of South Squirrel Hill jutted north on Forbes Avenue only to encompass the Maxon Towers in which the politician was then living—making her officially a resident of the working-class district. Then there is Penn Avenue, which for decades (and with a few major exceptions) acted as a veritable Berlin Wall separating White and Black Pittsburgh in the East End.

Inevitably, a discussion about what makes Pittsburgh neighborhoods so crucial will have to grapple with ethnicity and its often more problematic

A sliver of Brooklyn on Hobart Street in South Squirrel Hill. *Photograph by Cbail19, distributed under a CC-BY 2.0 license.*

A different perspective on Northumberland Street in North Squirrel Hill. *Photograph by Cbail19, distributed under a CC-BY 2.0 license.*

partner, race. When it comes to celebrating ethnic neighborhoods, there is the inevitable romance of food and language, of community parishes and festivals imported wholesale from the Old Country, whereas racially homogenous communities imply segregation, redlining and structural racism. In Pittsburgh, there is the complexity of how during the first half of the twentieth century, a neighborhood like the Hill District could host a veritable renaissance of Black American culture in terms of music and literature, but the vitality of this community was at the expense of Black Americans being fully appreciated, integrated and empowered within the wider city. Toker writes that the "day of the monolithic ethnic neighborhoods is over," and while it may be true that there is a glut of Asian restaurants on Forbes and Murray in Squirrel Hill, and nary a deli in sight, and that Bloomfield is as likely to host James Beard Award–nominated restaurants as it is red sauce joints, the racial boundaries in Pittsburgh are still abundantly obvious. Like any other major northeastern or midwestern city (Pittsburgh is sort of both), for both good and bad, ethnic neighborhoods were integral to the fabric and tenor of the metropolis. It's often obvious in the names of neighborhoods, even as demographics have changed: German Deutschtown, Irish Greenfield, Polish—well, Polish Hill. Then there is Italian Bloomfield and Morningside; Jewish Squirrel Hill; Hungarian Hazelwood; Ukrainian Southside; Polish Lawrenceville; African American Homewood, the Hill District and Lincoln-Larimer. Demographics have often changed, sometimes radically. During the Belle Epoque, East Liberty was a wealthy railcar suburb for the Scots-Irish Presbyterian aristocracy; then it became a middle-class hub for Italian and Jewish immigrants as well as Black southerners moving north during the Great Migration; next it became a redlined community that was de facto segregated and often the locus of discriminatory urban planning initiatives, having developed a reputation as being a slum; and now more recently it has, with some controversy, become a gentrifying, fashionable, in-demand area housing a burgeoning tech industry (Google has an office, and Duolingo's headquarters is here).

Pittsburghers of a certain age can remember experiences that were forged in the kiln of the city's ethnic neighborhoods. Enjoying buttery pierogis and greasy kielbasa at the Sokol Club on East Carson Street in the Southside; massive hoagies made with Mancini's bread and imported

The iconic steeple of East Liberty Presbyterian Church at night. *Wikimedia Commons, distributed under a CC-BY 2.0 license.*

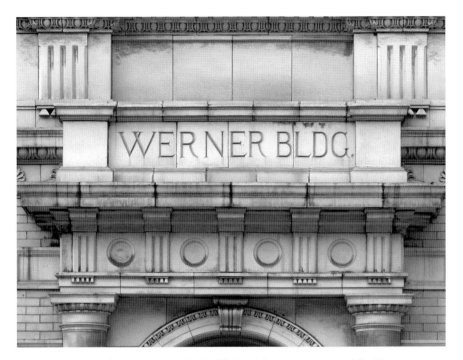

Exquisite Victorian molding on the South Highland Avenue entrance of the Werner Building, demonstrating East Liberty's once prodigious wealth. *Photograph by Father Pitt, distributed under a CC1.0 license.*

prosciutto, mortadella, capicola, provolone and hot peppers purchased at Groceria Merante in South Oakland; pastrami and Swiss on rye with hot mustard at Rhoda's, maybe with a scoop of astringent chopped liver, on Murray in Squirrel Hill; grabbing a few pints of Guinness at Kelly's in Regent Square; or maybe enjoying the fried catfish sandwich and hush puppies at the Crawford Grille while listening to a live jazz ensemble that could have included Ahmad Jamal or Art Blakey. Then there is the vitality expressed in things as varied as a poetry reading at City of Asylum in Allegheny West, a folk concert at the Gaslight Club in Shadyside, a punk band performing at Oakland's Electric Banana, a St. Joseph's Day parade in Bloomfield. Some of these experiences are still possible; sadly, many of them aren't. Pittsburghers will know which are which, but those examples I gave hopefully convey the breadth of these little atomized enclaves within the tightness of the city. As Jane Jacobs writes in her classic *The Death and Life of Great American Cities,* "Lively, diverse, intense cities contain the seeds of their own regeneration, with energy enough to carry over for problems and needs outside themselves," and even after a precipitous decline in population, the continued élan vital of Pittsburgh's neighborhoods is a running demonstration of that claim. Far more than geography, it's the character of the people that makes those ninety neighborhoods so discrete, distinctive, disparate.

A reality of Pittsburgh that sometimes surprises visitors is how *urban* it feels, unlike those massive, sprawling cities of the Southeast and Southwest that are effectively suburbs of themselves. Yet in ranking the largest cities in the United States, Pittsburgh is at a paltry 68, our 300,431 souls putting us only slightly above that nonmetropolis of Greensboro, North Carolina. At our largest, in 1940, Pittsburgh had 671,659 women, men and children—the ninth-largest city in the United States—having since experienced a decline of some 50 percent, which speaks to the sheer violence of deindustrialization. Obviously this isn't the whole story, though. If you examine a list of the *densest* cities in the United States—those are the places that feel like an actual a city and not a stretch of suburban strip malls in the Arizona desert or the tidewater South—Pittsburgh remains at number nine: slightly denser than Providence, Rhode Island, and almost exactly as dense as Washington, D.C. We share the top ten list with Boston, San Francisco, Philadelphia, Chicago and New York. In my family's firmly upper-middle-class neighborhood, I could hear the feminine robotic voice of the bus reading off the stop announcement as it picked up passengers on Penn Avenue. I could hear our next-door neighbor sneeze when he was inside his house (admittedly, he had cacophonous ones). Our current house is so close to my neighbor's that if I stand in the easement between them, I can easily touch both properties—and have to bend both my arms to do it. When I was in graduate school in the New York City metro area, there were lots of fellow students who lorded their Big Apple–dom, but most were from Long Island and Westchester County. Visiting Manhattan once a year because their parents spent an hour commuting into the city did not a New Yorker make, in my estimation. That's why I was honored when a good friend of mine, one of the only students actually from the five boroughs and a proud resident of Marine Park, said that she and I were the only colleagues from actual cities. She got it.

A large reason for Pittsburgh's relatively paltry size has to do with the bizarre way in which local government organizes municipalities. The population of Allegheny County is a whopping 1.238 million people, making it larger than Montana, Rhode Island, Delaware, both Dakotas and Alaska. *Yet Allegheny County has 130 municipalities*, among the largest number in the United States for a county of over a million people. The county is

The ninth-densest city in the United States, as seen in Lawrenceville. *Photograph by Pontzer98, distributed under a CC-BY 2.0 license.*

perhaps the most Balkanized of jurisdictions in the United States, maybe only rivaled by Suffolk County, Massachusetts, and the region is filled with cities, towns and boroughs that by any reasonable estimation should be in Pittsburgh proper. If such municipalities were anywhere else in the country, they would have long ago been incorporated into the city. If Pittsburgh and Allegheny County were to consolidate—the same process that has happened in countless cities across the United States—than suddenly we'd be vaulted back into the ninth place, unseating Dallas and right behind San Diego by just a few thousand.

"Annexation remains common in America's Sun Belt," writes former *Pittsburgh Post-Gazette* columnist Brian O'Neill in his book *The Paris of Appalachia: Pittsburgh in the Twenty-First Century,* but "in Pennsylvania it's history." Giving an overview of the various communities from Mount Washington to Lawrenceville that were gobbled up by Pittsburgh, not to mention the entirety of the massive north side Allegheny City, O'Neill advocates for the logic behind city-county consolidation. He writes that there is an innate logic in how "city and mill town and suburb might work together," as the "fragmentation of Allegheny County fosters an us-versus-them mentality...while the rest of America eats our lunch." Obviously he's correct, but the marriage of Pittsburgh's 90 neighborhoods with an additional 130 municipalities is hampered by inertia and unwillingness. There's also a sense—not entirely unreasonable—that places like rural West Deer Township are clearly not Pittsburgh, even if they happen to share a county (though Charlotte or Phoenix might not be so judicious in those distinctions). Regardless, there are places that are clearly Pittsburgh even if the residents don't pay city taxes or vote in local elections. Try explaining to somebody from out of town how they're not in Pittsburgh when they're

Douglas Cooper's 2017 *City of God*, showing Orthodox churches from the South Side. *Courtesy of Douglas Cooper.*

in Homestead, Wilkinsburg, Edgewood, Aspinwall, Sharpsburg, Millvale, Etna, Dormont or Mount Lebanon and witness the resulting confusion.

Partially it's because all those places, city neighborhoods and county mill towns, do share a presence of place, a kind of visual sense that's ultimately, finally and irrevocably Pittsburgh: a look, a feel, a disposition. Douglas

Cooper, professor of architecture at Carnegie Mellon University, has made Pittsburgh his muse much as Donoughe has. Yet while Donoughe celebrates the breadth of the region, Cooper returns to something elemental in his fantastical imaginings. The astounding two-hundred-foot mural that Cooper completed in 1996 for CMU's Skibo Hall replicates a sense of Pittsburgh that emerges beyond either literal time or space. While it technically depicts the campus of the university at three different periods, Cooper mingles both the historical and the contemporary into a singularity, where the nineteenth century and the twentieth fold in on each other as a Möbius strip (not unlike being in Pittsburgh itself, where the past is always so present). Soot ash and charcoal gray, the color of Pittsburgh clouds in February, Cooper's graphite unfolds along preposterously steep hillsides, wooden and brick rowhouses defying God as they cling above valleys and rivers, the undulating, unfurling of roads so confusing that it would take a topologist to understand their cracked geometry.

"The countless vantage points of the topographical city encourage the active perception of its visual qualities," writes Martin Aurand in *The Spectator and the Topographical City*, positing that part of what makes Pittsburgh unique are the various "rooms" that constitute it, made by water and earth. Hence the endless possibilities for dramatic skylines—the grandiose sweep of Downtown from Mount Washington and the explosion of the Golden Triangle as you arrive out of the Fort Pitt Tunnel, the stunning sweep as you approach from the north on I-79 and the neon sparkle on the *Capital Limited* train as you head west, Oakland's towers topped with neoclassical and neo-Gothic splendor, Bloomfield and Lawrenceville espied from the steep incline of Bigelow Boulevard appearing as if a medieval city crowding up to the castle of Children's Hospital, the rising spires of East Liberty and even the Rust Belt sprawl of Homestead. "In Pittsburgh, everyone is a spectator," notes Aurand. This is Cooper's vision, with the elemental nature of Pittsburgh's neighborhoods distilled into a gray but gorgeous wonderland. Within Cooper's mural there are the Victorian homes with their heavy wood and stained glass and the company houses in mill towns, the Gothic cathedral spires and the gleaming glass and rusty iron skyscrapers, the golden bridges and the charming inclines, the onion-domed churches and the smokestacks of the steel mills and always the flowing of the rivers, the stolidness of the mountains, the impermeability of the landscape, of nature. Even if the scene is imagined, it's clear that it could be nowhere other than Pittsburgh.

Chapter 3

EPISTLE TO STEELERS NATION

Not far from the Piazza Navona, with both Romans and tourists luxuriating in the rococo resplendence of the Fontana del Moro where a marble Neptune has overseen his watery Tritons since the sixteenth century, there is a charming trattoria in view of the Tiber River named La Botticella. If you were making your way through the Piazza Navona on a warm spring evening, the horizon beyond St. Peter's in the distance turning the color of melting orange gelato, past the diners at sidewalk tables enjoying piping plates of *cacio e pepe* and crispy *carciofi alla giudia*, squid-ink black tagliatelle and *spaghetti alla carbonara*, glasses of grappa and thimbles of espresso, chilled Negronis and smooth vermouth, you may elect to have a nightcap at that café on Via di Tor Millina. Ascending the steps into the dark, narrow bar, you see beautiful young Romans sipping golden Frascati or a small glass of Peroni, maybe eating some *suppli* purchased from a vendor in the piazza. At the counter of La Botticella, you may grab a drink from the proprietor, Giovanni Poggi, as you settle in and examine your environs: the small Italian flag posted on the liquor shelf behind the bar; the faux greenery affixed to the doorway, imparting a classically sylvian appearance to what's, after all, a pub of dark wood and red-tiled floors. There are arched doorways throughout the slender tavern, constructed with bricks that give them the appearance of the entrances to the ancient stadium of Domitian, which two millennia ago stood some hundred steps from La Botticella, the environs where gladiators and chariot racers once competed and entertained thousands of screaming fans. Appropriately,

The Colosseum in Rome, not far from the city's only Steelers bar. *Photograph by Diego Dieso, distributed under a CC-BY 2.0 license.*

Three Rivers Stadium in Pittsburgh, 1992. Of this iconic stadium and the two-millennia-old Colosseum, only one still stands. *Photograph by Steve Tiesdell, distributed under a CC-BY 2.0 license.*

there is a representation of another fabled stadium that still stands: a set of yellow hand cloths that Poggi sells behind the bar that depict the Colosseum, emblazoned black with the words *l'asciugamano terribile*: the Terrible Towel. That's when you notice it, in keeping with the delightfully profane reverence of the Romans: the baroque plaster painted statue of Jesus Christ with his glowing red sacred heart that stands guard at the middle of the bar's counter is wearing a black-and-gold American football helmet with the distinctive three diamonds known as hypocycloids in the middle of a circle. Appropriately enough, not far from Pittsburgh Jesus, as he is known, is a photograph of that great Italian Franco Harris. Here, you may be in the Eternal City, but you're also very much in Steelers Nation.

Steelers Nation is not just in Pittsburgh or McKeesport and New Kensington, Canonsburg and Washington, Wheeling and Youngstown but also at Pittsburgh Pete's in Largo, Florida; McMurphy's Sports Café in Rochester, Minnesota; Gabe's Bar and Grille in Los Angeles, California; Hibernia in Hell's Kitchen, Manhattan; Tortoise Bar and Grille in Arlington, Virginia (Iron City on tap); Giordano Brothers All-in-One Sandwiches in San Francisco (fries served on, not next to); and in more exotic locales such as the Famous Three Kings Pub in London, the Pittsburgh Bar and Diner in Belfast, Blozik's Blitzburgh Café in Sarajevo, El Torrito in Jalisco, Legends Sports Bar in Tokyo, the Big Bamboo Sports Bar and Grille of Shanghai, the Garden Bar in Bangkok and the Desert Eagle Lounge in Al Udeid Air Base, Qatar. According to curators Astria Suparak and Jon Rubin, who organized the exhibit *Whatever It Takes: Steelers Fan Collections, Rituals and Obsessions* at the Miller Institute of Contemporary Art at Carnegie Mellon University, there are "2,000 self-proclaimed Steelers bars and fan clubs worldwide, existing in every American state and over 25 different countries" across six continents, and presumably somebody in Antarctica has a Terrible Towel. While East Carson Street may indeed be long and densely packed with watering holes, it would nonetheless appear that the majority of the establishments flying Steelers flags and displaying photographs of Terry Bradshaw, Mean Joe Greene and Lynn Swann are not actually in Pittsburgh.

"Steelers country has no border," argues Mike Morlacci in an appreciation of La Botticella published in the *Pittsburgh Tribune Review*. Examining the map showing the location of every Steelers bar in the world as exhibited at the Miller would seem to confirm that contention. There are certain American cities that are celebrated throughout the world, as the neon Broadway dreams of Manhattan and the beachfront Hollywood fantasies of Los Angeles can confirm, but Pittsburgh's odd popularity is less expected. No other city of its size and history has quite the same popularity; it's hard to imagine a similar project mapping Cleveland Browns bars throughout the world (one wonders how many are even in Ohio) or a Detroit Lions bar on the Ponte Vecchio, yet for some inscrutable reason, the Three Rivers compels a magnetic attraction to many who wouldn't know the Al from the Mon, Shadyside from Morningside. Anyone from Pittsburgh who has traveled has had that uncanny experience of our relatively small city eliciting nods of recognition, often because of the Steelers, or the stories about seeing fans in Mexico City wearing Jerome Bettis jerseys or a girl in Seoul with a Hines Ward T-shirt, of that pub near Trafalgar Square with a painting of the Downtown skyline displayed near the front window. For some reason, Pittsburgh transcends Western Pennsylvania, this oft-forgotten metropolis resonating with people from Antigua to Zambia who've never seen a slag heap on the Monongahela or attended a Lenten fish fry in Homestead. Much of this undoubtedly has to do with the Steelers and their incredible success after that first Lombardi Trophy in '74, to be joined by five more. Being the historical best team only explains so much, however, as inspiring as their no-nonsense school of gruff football as presided over by three generations of the loyal Rooney family, stalwart old-school Irish American Catholics, might be. After all, the Steelers are tied with the New England Patriots for number of won pennants, and everybody resents the Patriots outside of New England (they don't even like them in Connecticut).

Maybe you grew up in Carrick or Shaler or Forrest Hills, and maybe now you're in Falls Church, Virginia, or Tampa, Florida, or Anaheim, California; maybe you moved when you were young after a parent lost their job when the mills started to close; maybe every game day, instead of a Commanders flag or a Buccaneers flag or a Rams flag, the black and gold flies in front of your house. Maybe that's true for the family down the street as well. And your kids, even if they've never been to Pittsburgh. Maybe a niece or nephew, a coworker's kid, a friend from work gave you a copy of this book because they know you're the "Pittsburgh Guy (or Gal)." Such an identity, such a powerful association with a team and with the region whose name that team bears, is derived from the "confluence of the demise of the economy and the steel industry and the rise of the team happening simultaneously," argues Rubin in an interview on the Miller Gallery's website, so that the "diaspora of the fans who were tied to the team emotionally but had to leave Pittsburgh… became their way of staying connected to the city." Throughout the United States, no "second favorite team" is more common than the Steelers, which speaks to the massive migration of people out of the metro area a generation

Myron Cope's Original Terrible Towel some 250 miles above the surface of the Earth on the International Space Station. *Photograph by Drew Morgan, distributed under a CC-BY 2.0 license.*

ago and their arrival in places like the Washington, D.C., suburbs and Southern California.

To even speak of a "diaspora" may seem histrionic, the term conjuring the Babylonian Captivity of the ancient Jews or the Romani migration from Rajasthan more than it does an economic downturn in a midsized American city, and yet the full extent of the population collapse in Pittsburgh was enormous, obscured in part by the economic rebound that the city was able to accomplish in a manner that places like Flint or Detroit never were. Between 1980 and 1984, the number of Pittsburgh workers in the steel industry fell by half; by the end of the decade, it had fallen by two-thirds; in the 1980s, the metropolitan area's population fell by a staggering 10 percent, with a net increase in population not happening until 2023. Some two hundred thousand women and men would leave the Pittsburgh area during this period. Writing in 1982, the labor reporter John Hoerr, in his beautiful classic *And the Wolf Finally Came: The Decline and Fall of the American Steel Industry*, describes the economic situation in Pittsburgh as an "immense tragedy," a whole region "drained of their life's blood." And so people left—they went to Virginia and Maryland, Florida and Georgia, Washington and Oregon, and they took their memories of Pittsburgh with them.

As for the years of the Steelers' first four Super Bowl wins, they were in 1975, 1976, 1979 and 1980, right at the moment that the furnaces in Rankin and Clarion were cooling, that the orange glow of Jones & Loughlin

Steelers quarterback Terry Bradshaw and Pirates left fielder Willie Stargell pose with workers at the Jones & Laughlin Steel Mill, 1979. *Courtesy of* Sports Illustrated.

and Edgar Thompson dimmed, that the smokestacks of the Southside began to come down. To become the undisputed greatest team in football representing a region right as it's in freefall is a special type of responsibility. "The Steelers galvanized Pittsburgh through its darkest days," write Tom O'Lenic and Ray Hartjen in *Immaculate: How the Steelers Saved Pittsburgh.* "The team provided the city's citizens with a source of pride they could embrace, a thread that kept the community fabric intact," so that instead of Pittsburgh's status as only a casualty of privatization, deregulation and rapacious greed on the part of the steel industry's owners, it could also be known as the "City of Champions" (it helped that the Pirates were actually good during those years as well). As a hypothesis, O'Lenic and Hartjen's claim has the feel of immutable truth to any Pittsburgh resident, here where Catholic priests wear black-and-gold stoles on game day and the world-class Symphony Orchestra has been known to go into an impromptu rendition of the Steelers fight song by the polka musician Jimmy Pol (born James Psihoulis).

Nowhere is more enmeshed in the sartorial options of black and gold, of Steelers and Pens jerseys, than if you're within the Three Rivers; walk down Liberty Avenue or East Carson Street or Smallman Street and a double-digit percentage of people will be wearing some kind of Pittsburgh swag. That sort of intensity radiates out from the city, but the glint of that gold still shines in many an exotic locale, in part a vestige of how extensive the diaspora of Pittsburghers is. Sportscaster John Facenda coined the term Steeler Nation in 1978 to refer to the fanbase for the team, but it quickly became representative of that wider exodus of residents forced to travel hundreds, if not thousands, of miles away from the forks of the Ohio to find new work somewhere else. Wright Thompson, a journalist for ESPN,

47

Left: Steelers victory parade for Superbowl XLIII in 2009 from the Boulevard of the Allies. *Wikimedia Commons, distributed under a CC-BY 2.0 license.*

Opposite: The most iconic picture of the Chief himself, Art Rooney Sr. *Wikimedia Commons, distributed under a CC-BY 2.0 license.*

wrote in a 2011 article about immigrants in Houston from the "nation-state of Pittsburgh," former steelworkers turned oil rig operators who get their pierogies and kielbasa in Polish delis and who grab a slice at a restaurant called Steel City Pizza. They and their children are of a "lost generation," writes Thompson, but the "connection, this idea of home, remained, feeling something like melancholy when they wrote 15224 on an envelope carrying pictures of their kids."

What should be obvious is that this isn't about the Steelers, or at least not only about the Steelers. The entire concept of Steeler Nation is bigger than football and something transcendent even of Pittsburgh, a longing for a place that used to exist but that has long since disappeared, just like the mills that used to proliferate across the landscape. "We're all from Pittsburgh," a transplant to Texas told Thompson; it's "just that the Pittsburgh that we're from isn't there anymore." Much of the national media, even decades after Big Steel's collapse, would use boilerplate filler when describing Pittsburgh, portraying it as a city of Bessemer converters and hot metal bridges long after the iron had cooled. Today, in a city whose population is growing, more Pittsburghers work for Google than they do U.S. Steel, and yet the old imagery endures, not least of all in the memories of those who left and the imaginations of those who came after them. Nostalgia, which can ever be a dangerous emotion, is at the root of much of this, but the Steeler Nation is representative of certain past arrangements that remain worth something, when labor was respected and it could be assumed that a certain level of comfort would be supplied to a family in exchange for the hard and necessary work that people did. Much of the connotations of Steeler Nation—the blue-collar toughness, the good-humored gruffness, the down-to-earth

 ballsiness—is, of course, inextricably connected to the team itself. This is in large part because of the Rooneys, who with their stolid, thoughtful and loyal model of no-tricks management reflect a particular old school approach to politics, culture and economics that's estimably alien in the dystopia dreamt up by folks at the Cato Institute and Hoover Institution. Art Rooney as depicted by the great Pittsburgh actor Tom Atkins in Gene Collier and Rob Zellers's play *The Chief* declares himself to be something rare, a "pro-labor Republican," and it's not just a funny line but an evocation of a fading Pittsburgh and a disappearing America in which working class values are actually respected and not just used as culture-war chum by billionaire faux populists. What the Steelers then represent to both Pittsburgh and its attendant diaspora is a particular approach to football—of working hard, of not being flashy, of sometimes relying on a bit of luck but having genuine gratitude for success. Of loyalty and class.

No variety of sports fandom in the United States is quite as fervent as Steelers fandom is. In a perceptive essay from 2013 for the religious studies magazine *Marginalia Review of Books*, Saint Francis University religion scholar Arthur Remillard writes, "With a creation narrative rooted in a miraculous event [the Immaculate Reception], a people scattered in other lands but bound to their homeland by a common creed, ethic, and dialect, and a sacred icon that springs forth a curse upon all who defile it [the Terrible Towel], Steelers Nation is a seriously religious place." Far from being glib or (only) a joke, Remillard's point is well taken. The love and, more importantly, the identification that people have with the Steelers clearly speaks to something beyond four quarters and 120 yards of gridiron. Like O'Lenic and Hartjen, Remillard argues that "Steelers Nation keeps an anchor in the city's blue-collar history, using every swirl of the Terrible Towel to connect the present with the past." For years, sportscasters have seemed to think that the sea of waving Terrible Towels at away games from Charlotte to Seattle evidence a propensity for Pittsburghers' willingness to drive across the continent, while ignoring the more obvious reality that these are former Pittsburghers, and the children of former Pittsburghers.

Steelers Nation is that mighty manifestation of the Pittsburgh diaspora, bowed but unbroken. That only partially explains the existence of Steelers

Nation, this *ummah* of Pittsburgh identity, for while it's less surprising that there are black-and-gold establishments in Bethesda or Boulder, those places relative geographic proximity to the Three Rivers doesn't help make sense of the Terrible Towels hanging on walls in Bratislava and Brasilia. May I suggest that O'Lenic and Hartjen's argument can also be reversed, that the Steelers didn't just supply a narrative for Pittsburghers to believe in themselves during the most dire years of economic collapse but that the Steelers also became a convenient metaphor for Pittsburgh itself, that in fact, the city supplied a bit of the narrative for the team? That obviously many love and root for and support the team even if they have no personal connection to the region because fans clearly revel in teams that win but that also such dedication to the Steelers may have something to do with a belief in Pittsburgh itself, even for those who've never been, even if it's a faith that's unconscious or intangible or mysterious? Sigmund Freud in *Civilization and Its Discontents* writes, "Let us suppose that Rome is not a place where people live, but a psychical entity with a similarly long and rich past," and now let us grab an Iron City at La Botticella and suppose the same of that other city built on seven hills.

Pittsburgh is a city in Western Pennsylvania, but Steelers Nation is something both larger and smaller—a fiction, a legend, a myth, a faith. While

The Steelers deep in enemy territory at the Cleveland Browns Stadium in 2019. *Photograph by Erik Drost, distributed under a CC-BY 2.0 license.*

the Pittsburgh of reality, the Pittsburgh that I live in, has changed sometimes for the worse but often for the better (and, increasingly, the latter), Steelers Nation is something more eternal. We're no longer the forge of American industry, the kiln of raw, brute manufacturing, mill for steel and glass, iron and coke. The lunch pail and hard hat memories aren't ours; they belong to our grandmothers and grandfathers. Now the sky is clear; there are stars at night (sometimes). The horizon is no longer orange; the smell of sulfur has dissipated. Our days, years and decades of being the arsenal of democracy and the engine of commerce are for history books and documentary films; the reality on the ground is entirely different, and nobody with any common sense would want the mills to reline the three rivers and begin belching their exhaust back into the cool Pittsburgh night. That's the blunt and irrevocable fact of it, regardless of the nostalgia. But Steelers Nation does represent something beyond reality, beyond history—and it represents something that's important and that must be held close.

Within Steelers Nation, there is a staunch adherence to community over the individual, to tradition over novelty, to connection and reciprocity over alienation and selfishness; there is an affirmation that good work deserves good pay and that the weekends are for tailgating and afternoon beers. In Steelers Nation, there may be some with a lot and many with little; there may be White and Black, Catholic and Protestant, Christian and Jewish. Differences are not erased in Steeler Nation, but for a few hours on any given Sunday, they might as well be, as briefly, everyone is from Pittsburgh. A common creed, a common identity, whereby all that other bullshit of the other six days of the week disappears, for a bit, on Sunday or Monday or Thursday. A Sabbath of belonging. In Steelers Nation, there is the bright, shimmering, incandescent possibility of creation, whether a touchdown or the communion of being with other fans, of that possibility spoken of by the poet Mauricio Kilwein Guevara in his lyric "Bright Pittsburgh Morning" from his collection *Poema*, wherein he describes how "I flip the welder's mask: / Sun off the rectangular glass, a rose glint before the white torch," and for a brief moment, we can imagine ourselves making something new once again.

Chapter 4

BRIDGES, INCLINES
AND PAPER STREETS

E very worthwhile city requires its symbols. They are the unique vocabulary through which a city tells stories about itself, both to those who live within it and to those who do not. Washington, D.C., is the Capitol Building and the White House, Los Angeles the Hollywood Sign and Sunset Boulevard, New York City the Statue of Liberty and the Empire State Building. Strictly speaking, when an image of that famed skyscraper is used to represent New York, it's not a metaphor but an instance of metonymy. Arguably, metonymy is a variety of internal metaphor, where rather than comparing two entirely different things, you conflate a large thing with something that is already a small constituent part of that larger thing. More generally, however, it's also clearly a symbol. There is an internal logic, a type of magic, whereby a place or a structure or an event comes to signify something much larger than itself. Cities may be literally built of concrete and steel, but they're truly constituted in the imagination, made of something else, of metaphor and metonymy, connotation and poetry. Of symbolism. Ralph Waldo Emerson writes in his essay "The Poet" that "we are symbols, and we inhabit symbols," and certainly Pittsburgh has been made a symbol of many things—industry, manufacturing, the working class—but it's composed of symbols, of a visual shorthand that expresses something ineffable about itself. When we walk on its bridges, ascend its paper streets, travel on the incline, we're taking part in overdetermined actions, in things that convey a certain *Pittsburghness* beyond the mundane reality of whatever it is that we're doing. "The myth is the collective dream of the people," writes the psychoanalyst Otto Rank in *The*

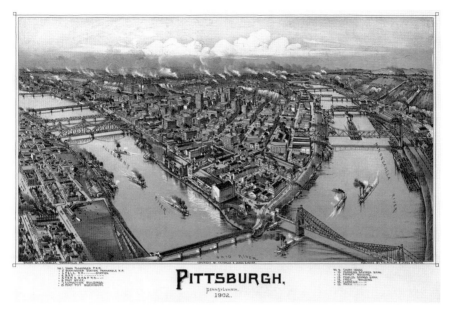

Cartographer Thaddeus Mortimer Fowler's 1902 depiction of Pittsburgh on the verge of its most spectacular industrial successes. *Distributed under a CC-BY 2.0 license.*

Myth of the Birth of the Hero: A Psychological Explanation of Myth, and it raises the question of what exactly our dreams are in Pittsburgh? When we imagine Pittsburgh, when we think of a shorthand of what this place is, what do we envision?

Martin Aurand observes in *The Spectator and the Topographical City* that Western Pennsylvania's "communities and neighborhoods are variously defined by hills and demarcated by hollows.…There are a great number and variety of contrivances for scaling, connecting, and otherwise negotiating the terrain, ranging from bridges to tunnels to inclined planes and public steps." What seems clear, at least to me, is that Pittsburgh's representative symbol must be the child of our material circumstances, a result of our terrain. So anecdotally and unscientifically, if I were to answer what most represents Pittsburgh, what poetic shorthand conveys the city in the same way a skyscraper embodies New York or a palm tree represents Los Angeles, what would I say? There's one obvious answer to that question. Nothing is as totemistic to Pittsburgh as bridges. Absent those bridges, Pittsburgh would be more archipelago of disconnected neighborhoods than continuous city, but that network of 450 (actually 446) not only makes it possible to cross the water to get from Downtown to the Northside or Oakland to the Southside but also connects land adjacent between Bigelow Boulevard and Bloomfield or the backend of Squirrel Hill to Greenfield.

Brady Smith writes in *Making History: The Heinz History Center Blog* that before the bridges were built, "Pittsburgh was a rugged terrain of deep valleys, creeks, and rivers, isolating many of the city's residents," though the joke still holds that residents won't bother traversing any of those bridges to get to a separate part of the city. If similarly hilly San Francisco has cable cars and the Golden Gate, then we've got what poet Jack Gilbert describes as "massive water / flowing morning and night throughout a city / girded with ninety bridges" (he was just numbering those that can be easily named). Omnipresent as a regional symbol—appearing on T-shirts advertising the Pittsburgh Bicentennial of 2016 or a new bougie apartment complex in Oakland called the Bridge on Forbes—is often some variation of a stylized black-and-gold arch from the Three Sisters, the bridge itself an instantly identifiable shorthand for Pittsburgh.

"As children, we were always told all these wonderful stories about the bridges," said the PEN/Voelker Award–winning poet Ed Roberson in an interview with *Callaloo*, "an industrially spectacular city.…People were always up to something, too. Everybody was always working at something, plugging away at building something." At least that was true at one point. Like Roberson, every person who goes through the Pittsburgh public schools, and probably then some, hears the factoid that no city in the world—not even Venice—has as many bridges as we do. And it's true, actually. Though it's surprisingly smaller than Pittsburgh, so per capita considerations need to be made, that mysterious Italian city of canals and gondolas, arabesque St. Mark's Basilica and the white latticework rococo of the Dodge's Palace, is bereft of some four dozen bridges when compared to us. While none of theirs are steel-girder golden suspension bridges, we've still copied one of

Pittsburgh's version of the Bridge of Sighs, as photographed in 1903. *Photograph by the Detroit Publishing Company, distributed under a CC-BY 2.0 license.*

Venice's iconic Bridge of Sighs. *Photograph by Antonin Contin, distributed under a CC-BY 2.0 license.*

Venice's more infamous crossings in the form of the Bridge of Sighs, which transported the condemned from their courtroom trial across a canal to their execution. Pittsburgh's Gothic granite version is over Grant Street (and nobody about to be executed walks on it anymore), because if we can't build a bridge over a river or a ravine, we'll put one over a road.

Over our three rivers, there's the Smithfield Street Bridge, a lenticular truss structure whose curved girders shaped like an infinity symbol are painted a celestial blue, connecting Downtown to the flats of Station Square before Mount Washington makes its abrupt and hurried steep ascent upward. The second-oldest steel bridge in the country, it was built to replace a previous structure that had been designed by John Roebling, the engineer who would go on to construct the Brooklyn Bridge, which was itself built after the city's first crossing, erected in 1818, was immolated in the Great Fire of 1845. Further east down the Monongahela is the Hot Metal Bridge, a preposterously stereotypical industrial truss bridge that used to transport molten iron crucibles between blast and hearth furnaces at the Jones and Loughlin steel mill; fully 15 percent of American steel passed over that bridge during the Second World War. Now it connects CMU computer science buildings to a shopping center on the south bank of the river. The triumphant Fort Pitt Bridge bursts forth from the tunnel on the mountainside

Two of the "Three Sisters" bridges visible from the third. These Allegheny River crossings are the only three identical self-anchored suspension bridges to appear in a single row anywhere in the world. *Photograph by Jet Lowe, distributed under a CC-BY 2.0 license.*

overlooking the skyline, a double-decked bowstring arch bridge where cars, trucks and buses suddenly have a view of the confluence of the three rivers and the Golden Triangle. On the Allegheny, there is the David McCullough Bridge, named after the local historian famous for his biographies *John Adams* and *Truman*, as well as for being the narrator of Ken Burns's *The Civil War*, though everybody still calls this steel trussed arch structure the Sixteenth Street Bridge, instantly recognizable by the massive astrolabe-like orbs announcing its entrance. Then there are the golden Three Sisters, self-anchored suspension bridges once known as the Sixth, Seventh and Ninth Street Bridges though renamed after baseball player Roberto Clemente, artist Andy Warhol and environmentalist Rachel Carson, respectively, three parallel, identical siblings glowing in incandescent beauty.

Less famous than our bridges but a result of the same uneven, crinkled and undulating terrain are our so-called paper streets. An outsider examining a map of Pittsburgh's confusing and curvy roadways—where a left isn't always a left, streets can change their name several times as they slither back in on themselves and two different grid patterns converge on Downtown to create a morass of odd diagonal corners—should be forewarned that oftentimes there are thoroughfares charted that aren't actually thoroughfares, inconvenient fictions of topography. Known as paper streets for the simple reason that they're only streets on paper, over 712 instances of them are maintained by the city, almost always as a set of perilously tall and steep concrete steps of varying degrees of preservation. For the intrepid motorist used to the broad, straight boulevards of Chicago or the Cartesian grid of Manhattan, the paper street is a surreal enigma, for even Google Maps is sometimes flummoxed by these cartographic remainders: a road you're driving on may suddenly end in a descending, crumbling concrete staircase that may or may

The Smithfield Street Bridge from Station Square looking north to Downtown. *Photograph by Cbail19, distributed under a CC-BY 2.0 license.*

not have a rickety, rusted railing helping any pedestrians get to the bottom of a hill on which said street continues, never bothering to change its name during that brief interlude—effectively an alleyway made from steps.

Fully sixty-six of Pittsburgh's neighborhoods can be crisscrossed by paper streets, helping those on foot get up and down the sides of the city's omnipresent steep hills, where vinyl-sided homes are set on cliffsides as if they were ancient pueblos but where, for at least a few blocks (or "blocks"), the American automobile's normally unchallenged dominion finds itself failing. Urban designer Frederick Law Olmstead Jr., son of the architect responsible for both Central Park and much of the National Mall, noted that "no city of equal size in America or perhaps the world, is compelled to adapt its growth to such difficult complications of high ridges, deep valleys, and precipitous slopes as Pittsburgh," a solution to which was the sublime fiction of the paper street, the rounding error of cartography. Pittsburgh isn't the only city to feature paper streets; San Francisco has its share, as does our partner on the Ohio River, Cincinnati, but neither have the sheer number that we do. They lie hidden in deep foliage, through the high-

Clarissa Street in the Upper Hill District. *Photograph by Laura Zurowski, distributed under a CC-BY 2.0 license.*

ridged peaks of the North Side's neighborhoods and the sheer fall of Mount Washington, deep in the valleys that act as Oakland's basement and through the perilously steep dwellings of the West End. Pittsburgh is like a metropolis dreamt of by a world-building fantasy writer, the sheer improbability of its existence responsible for many of these aspects of the city. Its paper streets are far less famous outside of the region than its bridges are—bluntly, they're not very photogenic by themselves—but they function as hidden wormholes connecting the peaks with the flats, threading together disparate neighborhoods that would otherwise be isolated to the ambulatory pilgrim of Pittsburgh's peaks and valleys.

Bob Regan, in his book *Pittsburgh Steps: The Story of the City's Public Stairways*, brags that "geologically speaking there is no other city in the world like Pittsburgh," with its dramatic vistas crafted not by plate tectonics but only by erosion, a region he describes as "physiographically challenged." Enumerating the many ways in which Pittsburghers have historically dealt with their difficult geography, from inclines to bridges, tunnels to trolleys, Regan concludes that "undoubtedly the city steps are the most unique of these transportation solutions." Paper streets are arguably a Pittsburgh secret; they're not very pretty—neither majestic in the way that the bridges are or charming as the incline is—but they do have their own idiosyncrasy that's not worth discounting. Besides, while they're rarely worth looking *at*, they're frequently worth looking *from*. Predictably, the bulk of paper streets tend to be in more working-class neighborhoods (though that's not an inviolate principle), but in a city where smog meant visibility was nonexistent everywhere, there was no compunction about lining the ridges of hills with

Pittsburgh's skyline at night as seen from Mount Washington. *Wikimedia Commons, distributed under a CC-BY 2.0 license.*

Oakland's equally dramatic skyline, in its neoclassical and Gothic splendor. *Wikimedia Commons, distributed under a CC-BY 2.0 license.*

affordable homes that, in other locales, would be on plots selling for hundreds of thousands, if not millions, of dollars. The result is that walking up a paper street that cuts through a dense overgrowth of green foliage in a blighted neighborhood can result in suddenly being able to see a hidden but sweeping Downtown skyscraper view, the city emerging from all that forestry as if a conjured chimera, a dream metropolis appearing from where before there was undifferentiated nothing.

For example, there is the vista presented to you from the St. Thomas Street stairs in the Allentown neighborhood just over the crest of Mount Washington; or the intersection of the Northside's often-bustling James Street, which momentarily transforms into a set of concrete steps; or Graib Street in the appropriately named neighborhood of Fineview, a community christened for what you can see not within its confines but from them. Residents can have a feeling of proprietary ownership over these steps— sometimes actual ownership as well, for the law is frequently ambiguous about whose responsibility the paper streets are—as they are hidden tunnels cutting through nature, linking the various hillside islands of the Pittsburgh archipelago. A renter on Airbnb offers a two-hour tour of paper streets (it has five stars), while Patrick Doyle, a transplant to the city and staunch advocate for Pittsburgh, has developed his own affection for this odd feature of our terrain, founding an online database dedicated to the phenomenon entitled PGH Paper Streets. "Paper streets are like unfinished thoughts," writes journalist Emily DeMarco in *Public Source*, and it's a beautiful metaphor. Consider Frazier Street in South Oakland, the neighborhood above the valley marked by long university buildings and multistoried towers, by neon and traffic—but then this imaginary street of concrete steps that cuts down through the foliage of the hillside, disappearing into ivy-covered nature like the ruins of a lost civilization.

More than the paper steps, or even the bridges, our most iconic physical symbol is arguably the Duquesne Incline, two wood-paneled Victorian railcars that each fit around eighteen people and are painted a joyful red with yellow trim about the windows, looking like a pair of Christmas presents moving in opposite directions as they descend and ascend the 793 feet of track from Station Square to the top of Mount Washington, some five hundred feet up, at a geometrically impressive thirty degrees, moving a casual four miles per hour, all on an unusual five-gauge rail. So regular is the everyday scene of these little red cars slowly making their trip up the side of a mountain looming over the skyscrapers of Downtown that your average Pittsburgher probably doesn't reflect on how deeply weird, wondrous, fantastic and fabulous such a view is. The Duquesne Incline, like the bridges it travels above, is a convenient symbolic shorthand for Pittsburgh, displayed on welcome posters at the airport and in advertisements for hospitals, as well as almost certainly being the inspiration for the trolley that travels to the Neighborhood of Make Believe in *Mister Rogers' Neighborhood*, a delightful and understated weirdness of Pittsburgh's landscape that exists nowhere else in the country. Cheerful, plucky and indomitable, the little red funicular has made its journey every day of the year since 1877 when it was designed by the Hungarian engineer Samuel Diescher, built to transport miners on what was then known as Coal Hill. The Duquesne was originally one of seventeen funiculars throughout Pittsburgh; only it and its substantially less photogenic sibling, the Monongahela Incline, a bit farther down Grandview Avenue, still operate. The Duquesne Incline itself barely survived, its continued operation only ensured because of the foresight of community groups in the early 1960s that prevented the stations and rail from being destroyed. It endures as a quintessentially Pittsburgh experience, the railcar on its steep incline juxtaposed with the autumnal reds, oranges and browns on Mount Washington, with the vast sweep of Downtown across the river.

An absurdly Pittsburgh scene from the Duquesne Incline. *Photograph by Dllu, distributed under a CC-BY 2.0 license.*

Over a million people travel on the incline every year, many of them tourists, though a substantial number are workers making their daily commute, for just $2.50 paid to Port Authority Transit. Visitors at the top station are greeted by a refreshingly low-tech exhibition, a waiting room with a gift shop selling mugs and postcards, a window that allows views of the massive-spoked red gears turning the cables and a counter with a few snacks for sale (all cash; exact change required for travel). Within the tiny car itself—slightly rickety, smelling of old wood, with a hard bench running around its internal perimeter and a gorgeous hammered copper ceiling— there are unparalleled views of Pittsburgh's skyline. For all the charm of the incline itself, that's what really makes it so celebrated: this perspective of Downtown both from within its car and at the top of Mount Washington itself. It's been the site of countless prom, engagement and wedding photos (surely, in old-fashioned Pittsburgh, some of those three categories have the same two people in them from start to finish). *USA Today* in a 2013 article described it as the second most beautiful view in America, only after the Grand Canyon. That dramatic panorama was crafted by God, whereas Pittsburgh is at least a collaboration.

"The rivers cup downtown's lustrous Golden Triangle, where landmark skyscrapers thrust upward like rockets," reads the unsigned article. "At nights, lights twinkle on no fewer than 15 bridges." The judges (correctly) decided that all this was more beautiful than the Golden Gate Bridge (number 5), Key Largo (number 8) or the antebellum Spanish moss–covered squares of Savannah, Georgia (number 10). More even than the funicular itself, it's the skyline that is so iconic, so totemistic, so symbolic of Pittsburgh, that view from the Fort Pitt Tunnel or approaching the city from the north on I-79 or from the window of the Duquesne Incline itself. It's a view so beautiful—in the sweep of the hills, the drama of the rivers, the marvel of the skyscrapers, framed either by a low rumble of clouds moving in on a summer night or the crispness of a moonlit winter evening—that any fair aesthetic appraisal would have it that none of us deserve something that looks like this, that Pittsburgh doesn't even deserve it. On Grandview Avenue—with the wind rushing in across the valley, high-peaked and facing north; the grandeur of the skyline, thousands of those twinkling lights brighter than any mere star, the neon glowing with more luminescence than the paltry moon; the flow of the rum-black rivers; and the homes clinging to the cliffside beyond—for a second, at least, it can feel as if all of it is worth it, despite any ugliness or heartbreak, inequity or injustice, grittiness or filth, all of that merely the cost of beauty in our fallen world.

Characteristic Pittsburgh domestic stained glass window, here at the Brayton Apartments in Shadyside. *Photograph by Father Pitt, distributed under a CC1.0 license.*

Ultimately, though, when looking for a symbol of Pittsburgh, or at least a secret glyph known to us residents, not called on for news broadcasts or insurance advertisements, the bridges and the inclines must fall short, not least of all because few people live on the former and even fewer on the latter. For me, the symbol of Pittsburgh must be entirely more personal. If a sense of place can't be reduced to a simple icon, to golden bridge or red incline, then more appropriately, there are a few hundred thousand individual symbols of Pittsburgh in the form of the homes and houses, apartments and condominiums throughout the city. There are the stereotypical iron city working-class rowhomes of red brick or the aluminum-sided single-family homes that proliferate not just in reality but in depictions of the region, but there is also a preponderance of residences built from the end of the Gilded Age through the beginning of the Great Depression: the Gothic, Tudor, Victorian and Craftsman styles throughout Shadyside and Squirrel Hill, Point Breeze and Friendship that are characteristically evocative of Pittsburgh. Toker describes these gorgeous homes with "original ornamental woodwork, polished hardwood floors, and stained-glass windows," preserved for more than a century, instantly recalling the period at which Pittsburgh was in its ascendancy. There is a distinct appearance to a Pittsburgh home, the region an architectural isolate preserving beautiful styles and designs in buildings that in other municipalities were torn down or demolished during periods of renewal.

Now, with our fortunes at least partially preserved, the heavy wood detailing and stained glass of many a century-old Pittsburgh home remains, left untouched while other cities erased so much craftsmanship and detail in favor of postmodern cheapness and bland uniformity. In anticipation of my family moving back to Pittsburgh, we attended dozens of open houses (always fun), and I was horrified as I heard Silicon Valley tech bros and northern Virginia lanyards talk about ripping out stained glass and sandblasting the Gothic-black grit from stone. For my own design aesthetic, I adhere to the French philosopher Gaston Bachelard, who in his study *The Poetics of Space* rather beautifully argues that the "house shelters day-dreaming, the house protects the dreamer, the house allows one to dream in peace." When contemplating the intricate puzzle-like luminosity of a stained-glass window with its heavy lead panes, sunlight shining orange and purple and green and casting the glow of a simple flower on a century-old dark-stained oak floor in an otherwise modest home, then I know that what I've found is a shelter for daydreaming, a protection for daydreaming, a deep-seated peace of something understood.

Chapter 5

HOLLYWOOD ON THE MON

Of all John Wayne's roles, from the stoic rancher in *The Man Who Shot Liberty Valance* to the crotchety sheriff in *True Grit*, few parts were as unlikely as that of the self-made coal miner turned millionaire Charles Markham in the largely forgotten 1942 film *Pittsburgh*. Directed by Lewis Seiler, *Pittsburgh* was about a bootstrapper who through guile, grift and gumption ascended the heights of the city's aristocracy. Also starring Marlene Dietrich as romantic interest Josie "Hunky" Winters (the nickname was a common slur against Eastern European mill workers) and, in a surprising bit of casting, Shemp Howard (of Three Stooges fame) as a tailor swindled by Markham, *Pittsburgh* was promoted as a "drama as fiery as a blast furnace." A lopsided Horatio Alger narrative, *Pittsburgh* is a rags-to-riches-back-to-rags-maybe-back-to-riches story, with Wayne's character first abandoning his friends while getting rich, then justly losing all of it, only to find redemption by starting again at the bottom, working to produce steel for the U.S. military during the Second World War. It's a movie about "forging a city's greatness… [and] a nation's power," as the trailer enthused. Not a particularly subtle bit of wartime propaganda, *Pittsburgh* was a critically panned box office hit (its reputation hasn't improved over the last eighty years), yet it still tells us something about both American industry and the city the film was named after. That Markham's nickname is Pittsburgh makes him a stand-in for the city, representative of all American industry. Wayne's character is greedy and hardworking, ambitious but tough and, finally, willing to do the right thing. A celebration of a certain economic and political order, Seiler's film depicts management and labor working together in their patriotic duty as paragons of New Deal liberalism. It's a simple movie with a simple title: the very name *Pittsburgh* told audiences all that they needed to know.

No other U.S. city is as symbolic of industry as is Pittsburgh—not Cleveland, not Chicago, not even Detroit, a situation that has led to the area becoming a cinematic shorthand. While each of those city's names connotes commerce—whether stockyards or automobile factories—"Pittsburgh" remains a catchall representing all U.S. industry, despite its economic collapse nearly half a century ago. Partially because Western Pennsylvania manufacturing was diversified in iron, aluminum, copper, natural gas, petroleum, glass, paint and food canning, and partially because Big Steel is so connected to the grit, filth and labor of production, the name of the city has long endured as a metaphor in a manner that those of other places haven't. There's an irony to the continued symbolic importance of "Pittsburgh," decades after free market policies gutted the region.

There is the actual city of Pittsburgh, and then there is the charged *Pittsburgh* of myth, a signifier of variable meaning depending on who is using it and why. Tinseltown meets the Steel City when the former is in need of using myths of the latter, for if the film industry is anything, it's a kiln and forge of fantasy, and Pittsburgh can be an intrinsic element in the production of that commodity. In the seventy-plus years since the movie *Pittsburgh* was released, the city has remained a stand-in on the silver screen for the same values expressed by Seiler's forgotten film, as well as unexpectedly become its own soundstage for other celluloid fantasies. Among the earliest films made in Pittsburgh were short silent reels documenting industrial production, movies with scintillating titles such as *Assembling a Generator*, *Coil Winding Section E* and *Testing Large Turbines*, all of which were screened with a dozen or so others as part of the Westinghouse Electric Corporation's pavilion at the 1904 St. Louis World Fair. For what they lack in pure thrills, nobody could accuse them of not selling a particular image of Pittsburgh—grimy and industrious, hardworking and gritty—which is still often the image being sold today. During the Golden Age of Cinema, when both the economics of the studio system and the prudishness of the Hayes Code constrained creativity, Pittsburghers still had an opportunity to see more sophisticated productions that depicted the city, albeit ones that often told the contours of a familiar story. Nor was Pittsburgh itself particularly distant—at least metaphysically—from Hollywood.

As much as the film industry in the region has grown over the past thirty years, encouraged by variable terrain for filming, the successful lobbying

John Wayne and Marlene Dietrich touted featured in this film poster for 1942's *Pittsburgh. Wikimedia Commons, distributed under a CC-BY 2.0 license.*

of the Pittsburgh Film Office and, of course, the lure of ever-enticing tax incentives, the city's film industry isn't a new phenomenon. John Tiech in *Pittsburgh Film History: On Set in the Steel City* explains how not only was the city the location for the first nickelodeon in 1905—effectively the first actual movie theater, located on Smithfield Steet—but also "film exchange buildings were constructed along the Boulevard of the Allies, a section of Pittsburgh known as 'film row,'" where studio owners, producers and theater managers could rent and trade upcoming features. Paramount's film exchange building was the last to close in 1970, but the actual structure still stands on the Bluff overlooking the Monongahela, marked by its former owner's distinctive mountainside logo. Most amazingly given the little amount of commemoration it receives, working-class Jewish Pittsburgh was the environment in which the influential, powerful, controversial and feared Hollywood producer David O. Selznick was born, a man responsible for both *Rebecca* and *Gone with the Wind.* Nor is that Pittsburgh's only connection to early Hollywood, for it was the distribution company Duquesne Amusement and Supply, founded in 1904, that would later move to California and transform into the famed studio named for its founders: Warner Brothers. The only studio during the Golden Age to be owned by New Deal Democrats, Warner Brothers developed a reputation for working-class cinema, arguably inculcated by its owners' years in Western Pennsylvania.

By 1939, audiences could enjoy *Allegheny Uprising*, also directed by Seiler and starring Wayne, a rare movie in which the Duke wears a coonskin cap, a problematic tale of settler-colonists fighting the Indians on the 1760s frontier. Two years later, director Jack Townley's *The Pittsburgh Kid* starred the local and beloved Irish Catholic heavyweight champion Billy Conn in a lightly fictionalized account of his ongoing boxing career. *Valley of Decision*, meanwhile, turned toward Gilded Age mythmaking: this 1945 Tay Garnett flick starring Gregory Peck is about the romance between the son of an 1870s millowner and his Irish maid, their love marked by the possibility of a labor strike. All these films offered a particular narrative of the region—as tough, industrious and working class and yet a place where the proletariat was always amenable to the dictates of capital (regardless of the historical reality).

Nor did Pittsburghers lack venues in which to screen said films; audiences could watch films like *Allegheny Uprising*, *The Pittsburgh Kid* and *Valley of Decision* in the red velvet–seated and gilded resplendence of the Loew's and United Artists Penn Theater with its Venetian ceiling and marble staircase; or the former Vaudeville house the Gayety Theater, adorned with rococo

Left: The first movie theater in the United States, on Smithfield Street. *Image courtesy of the Pittsburgh Cultural Trust.*

Right: Corporate symbol on Paramount's abandoned screening room, last remnant of the "Film Row" that once lined the Boulevard of the Allies. *Photograph by Lee Paxton, distributed under a CC-BY 2.0 license.*

ceiling murals of beautiful, bare-breasted muses floating above the screen; or the Stanley Theater, which sat four thousand people (all have since been preserved by the Pittsburgh Cultural Trust as live performance spaces), fantasies of Pittsburgh projected on celluloid several stories tall. Steven J. Ross describes in *Working-Class Hollywood* how such institutions targeted "skilled workers (and their families) and the growing amorphous middle class," the latter of whose members were often the "white-collar offspring of blue-collar families who had grown up watching movies in nickelodeon and neighborhood theaters." Pittsburghers watching Pittsburgh stories in Pittsburgh theaters, though, with few exceptions, shot on a Los Angeles sound stage.

Not that that remained a permanent situation, for any eagle-eyed Pittsburgher watching movies with friends can be known for shouting and pointing when a familiar location suddenly appears on screen. Thousands of films and television shows have been made in the city, so that cinephiles can spot Hannibal Lector's courthouse prison from *Silence of the Lambs* (1991) at the Soldiers and Sailors Memorial Hall; the Downtown skyline as espied from the Mon in *Groundhog Day* (1993); Grady Trip's Friendship front porch in *Wonder Boys* (1999); Kennywood's Steel Phantom rollercoaster in *Adventureland* (2009) and the adolescent adrenaline triumph of emerging from the Fort Pitt Tunnel in *The Perks of Being a Wallflower*, not to mention wide swaths of appropriately Gothic Oakland and the Golden Triangle transformed into Batman's Gotham for *The Dark Knight Rises* (the last two are both 2012).

Now the Benedum Center for the Performing Arts, this was once the Stanley Theater, which opened in 1928 with seating for 3,800 people. *Photograph by PerryPlanet, distributed under a CC-BY 2.0 license.*

Then, obviously, there's the immaculate cheese of Steel City action movies, from Jean-Claude Van Damme in *Sudden Death* (1995) as the least likely veteran of the Pittsburgh Police battling a nefarious Powers Booth, an extortionist who's taken thousands of Penguins fans in the Civic Arena hostage in what's effectively *Die Hard* during hockey overtime, to the original John McClaine himself, Bruce Willis, who plays a Pittsburgh river cop who goes his own way when trying to apprehend the Polish Hill stranger in the utterly ridiculous *Striking Distance* (1993)—though it does contain Chicagoan Sam Farina, who in a not-un-Pittsburgh growl declares the incontrovertible advice: "Take Bigelow, it's faster." Enumerating all the ways in which the hills and rivers, the stately buildings and decaying mills have been framed by directors in films where Pittsburgh may or may not be itself is a task for the film office, so surprisingly ubiquitous has the region's presence become in everything from action pablum, as with *Jack Reacher* (2012), to Academy Award–winning prestige flicks like *Fences* (2016), feel-good biopics such as *It's a Beautiful Day in the Neighborhood* (2019), saccharine romcoms like *Happiest Season* (2020) and prestige cable television drama like *American Rust* (2021) that

Jennifer Beal in *Flashdance. Image courtesy of Getty Images.*

there is barely anything all that notable anymore about seeing a decaying mill by a brown riverside or a shot of the PPG and U.S. Steel Building with the Batmobile flying overhead. Before any of them, though, there was just a Steel Town girl on a Saturday night...

Flashdance, it must be said at the outset, is not a good movie (though perhaps it's a great one). Adrian Lyne's 1983 blockbuster stars Jennifer Beal as a sexy welder/stripper who enters into a passionate love affair with Michael Nouri as the owner of the mill that employs her, all while harboring dreams of dancing for the Pittsburgh Ballet—basically Garnett's *Valley of Decision* with PG-13 stripping and a disco soundtrack by Irene Cara. The acting is either wooden or histrionic, the dialogue is both flat and melodramatic and the plot is very, very stupid (a friend of mine's father who worked as a welder was scandalized by the lack of proper OSHA safety protocols in the mill scenes). This, it should be remembered, is the movie that helped make producer Jerry Bruckheimer a household name. Notably, Roger Ebert included it in his list of Most Hated Films—comparing it unfavorably (but not unfairly) to *Saturday Night Fever*—while forty years later, it still only garners a paltry 35 percent on Rotten Tomatoes (no diamond in the rough, or gem in the rust, as it were). Noting how *Flashdance* was filmed, ironically, at the precise moment in which the steel industry was in collapse, the feminist critic Kathryn Kalinak argues in a contemporary essay from *Jump Cut: A Review of Contemporary Media* that *Flashdance* "acknowledges the exigencies of economic necessity while retaining the [musical] genre's democratic message," though she also rightly asks, "How could an 18-year-old woman land a skilled labor job as a welder in the unionized steel industry of an economically depressed union town? How could anyone?" *Flashdance* offered a fantasy of a Pittsburgh economic juggernaut that in reality was not just in eclipse but in apocalypse. Part of what has always personally drawn me to *Flashdance* is that it's a relic of Pittsburgh from the year before I was born, a portrait of a much larger city than the one I would end up being raised in. Filmed on location at places like the Carrie Blast Furnace, *Flashdance* is the last record of what was a fading order.

Despite all that, regardless of the hokum and schmaltz, maybe even because of it, *Flashdance* was an integrally important film to Pittsburgh identity, though it often traded in self-seriousness and cliché (though so do we all). Even Kalinak notes that movies have a "relation to the dream state, they have a unique power over us," where dreams and fantasy can be stronger than mere iron and steel. Beals's character is young and beautiful, hip and free, and rather than a rusty, dying town, Pittsburgh is dynamic, seemingly poised to be reborn. As she bikes up and down the steep streets of the city,

Ruins of the Carrie Blast Furnace in Rankin. *Photograph by Adam Jones, distributed under a CC-BY 2.0 license.*

the scaffolding of the U.S. Steel Tower and the Mellon Building rising behind her, the excellent cinematography of Donald Peterman presents a lushly gorgeous city. Beal is depicted dancing past the autumnal trees in front of the main branch of the Carnegie Library, looking out the window of the Duquesne Incline, even welding with sparks of molten metal framing the brunette curls billowing behind her mask (OSHA violations be damned): the fantasy offered by *Flashdance* is primally irresistible. Kalinak describes the film as valorizing the "energy of the chic, young, urban lifestyle," all of it pushed by the propulsive pop score of Cara (shockingly forward-thinking, it's the first major film to feature a hip-hop song). *Flashdance* is the antidote to *The Deer Hunter* (1978), a horrifying tale of Mon Valley working-class Ruthenian mill workers whose friendship takes them from Clairton to the war prisons of Vietnam, clearly a far better film in every single respect than Lyne's schlock but also a movie that's deeply reactionary in its sentiments and myths, lacking the utopian yearnings of *Flashdance*. If such a romance as *Flashdance* had little reality in 1983, the movie at least attempted to will it into being, and it's been sort of, kind of, maybe halfway successful. Because when "I hear the music, close my eyes, feel the rhythm wrap around, take ahold of my heart," then, well, what a feeling.

However, when it comes to the most radical of innovations in not just establishing a film industry in Pittsburgh but also, more generally, inventing an entirely new idiom of cinema, the story of movies here can be summed up in two words: George Romero. There had arguably been nothing quite like Romero's 1968 *Night of the Living Dead* before its premiere. That iconic opening scene in the country graveyard where actress Judith O'Dea is teased by her brother with the line "They're coming to get you, Barbara!" shortly before the resurrected dead did precisely that. What follows that initial taunt is ninety-six minutes of a small cast of survivors huddled together in a rural farmhouse as the dead relentlessly push at the windows and doors and boards of the dwelling, without conscience or consciousness but with only a deep, unceasing, cannibalistic hunger. In making this horrifying, gruesome, profane, satirical horror flick with a distinctly progressive social conscience, the director completely reinvented an entire cinematic genre and perhaps gave us the first distinctly American monster in the form of the Romero zombie. With *Night of the Living Dead*, Romero removed the zombie mythos from those origins that had assumed a sort of magical intention and placed the new zombie in an utterly amoral and nihilistic (and thus all the more horrifying) reality. Romero's was a vision owed not to Poe and his Gothic sensibility but rather to the amoral

From the trailer for *Night of the Living Dead*, 1968.

void of Lovecraft's weird tales, for "when there's no more room in hell, then the dead will walk the earth."

Pittsburgh was the city that incubated Romero's weird vision, and though he was a Cuban kid from the Bronx, Romero made Pittsburgh his own, and the city took to its adopted auteur. Romero's best work has a particularly Pittsburgh sensibility. Take *Martin* (1977), Romero's first collaboration with genius makeup artist Tom Savini (and the director's favorite film he made). An underappreciated masterpiece, *Martin* explores the dinginess of Pittsburgh right before the collapse of the steel industry, and it is intimately attuned to the old-world superstitious rhythms of the region, a combination that makes it an excellent example of that underexplored but potent and fertile genre: Pittsburgh Gothic. *Martin* follows the arrival of its titular character, who believes himself to be a vampire, to Pittsburgh, where he is to lodge with his Lithuanian Catholic grand-uncle Tateh Cuda (incidentally, Romero's mother was Lithuanian). Cuda agrees that his nephew is a vampire and sees it as his family responsibility to allow Martin to room with him, while it's his religious responsibility to prevent the vampire from feeding—which, of course, he does. This vampire drugs his victims by syringe, a serial rapist who

The master himself, George Romero, at the Venice International Film Festival in 2009. *Wikimedia Commons, distributed under a CC-BY 2.0 license.*

drinks blood, stalks his victims through the midnight streets of Pittsburgh and uses the name the Count to call in to a local advice DJ. With the brilliant dead-eyed performance of John Amplas, the spiritual world of *Martin* is completely ambiguous, for as the "vampire" informs the call-in listeners, "There's no real magic…ever." As with Martin Scorsese's *Taxi Driver* (1976), which uses an unreliable narrator with an inflated ego to explore the epistemic uncertainty that can accrue on a diseased consciousness, viewers of *Martin* are left to speculate if he really is a vampire or merely a delusional sociopath. If there were any justice, *Martin* would be seen as an exemplary New Wave character sketch and not "just" a genre film, and it would have inspired filmmakers to reinvent the vampire in the same way that the *Dead* franchise reinvented the zombie.

Or for another example, the underrated fourth film in Romero's zombie franchise, *Land of the Dead* (2005). Set in the same universe as the original trilogy, *Land of the Dead* is a prescient parable of our current United States, envisioning Pittsburgh as a surviving encampment of humans after the zombie apocalypse, the bridges of the three rivers bricked up and a series of walls blocking off the eastern boundary of the Golden Triangle, where the survivors are protected from the undead but ruled over by a sort of uber-rich feudal lord named Kaufman (deliciously played with Rumsfeldian efficacy by Dennis Hopper). In this Pittsburgh, the rich live in an imagined skyscraper named Fiddler's Green, while the majority scrounge around in the trash-strewn streets of what used to be Downtown, until an invasion by the increasingly sentient zombies threatens to turn upside down the unequal dystopia Kaufman has created. Threaded through the film are indications of Pittsburgh's particular class politics, for in a city of, historically, such inequity, there is an awareness of the contradictory reality of the robber barons who built this place in the nineteenth century, a city where seemingly everything is named Carnegie, Frick, Mellon, Heinz or Westinghouse but where you both love and hate Carnegie, Frick, Mellon, Heinz and Westinghouse. I was visiting a college girlfriend in Baltimore when I first saw the movie—my first Romero movie, I should say—and instantly picked up on the distinctly Pittsburgh tells, from the obvious (the maps and skyline were clearly the city) to the more tongue-in-cheek (the zombies, like Pittsburghers at a Zambelli display, are fixated by fireworks). Manohla Dargis, in a review for the *New York Times*, provincially noted that *Land of the Dead* took place in "a city with more than a passing resemblance to Manhattan," but I knew better.

Because before Hollywood on the Mon, what Romero offered to a horror movie–obsessed teenager living in pre-hipster Pittsburgh was the opportunity to see the dark humor and sensibility of the city presented on screen to a national audience. From the running list of Western Pennsylvania locations that scrolled at the bottom of the newscast in that first movie in the franchise to the Yinzer accent of local weatherman William "Chilly Billy" Cardille (who had a cameo as himself), the *Dead* franchise is Pittsburgh through and through, and the strange, misanthropic comedy of the films is distinctly of the region. A lot of Pittsburghers have dwelled in that contradictory psychology, simultaneously loving and hating those old bastards whose wealth made the city important while also being aware of their often-profound malignancy. It's an awareness that their money, which made a degree of comfort and sophistication possible in Pittsburgh, was also made on the backs of the people who actually lived here. Yet that wealth, in large part, is also problematically part of why the city shakily endured while large parts of the rest of the Rust Belt fell into economic disarray, like a fortified oasis in the midst of a zombie apocalypse.

Now, ironically, Romero joins that pantheon of undead industrialists with their names on buildings; the film industry here is arguably the direct result of the popularity generated by his zombie franchise. According to *Movie Maker* magazine, in 2022, Pittsburgh was ranked the fourth-best metropolitan area for filmmaking in the United States; the industry locally employs thousands and, in the last decade, has brought in over a billion dollars of tax revenue. Gushing over Pittsburgh as the new postindustrial Hollywood, Tim Molloy in *Movie Maker* describes the city as boasting "architecture that begs to be filmed, rolling hills, countless bridges crossing its three rivers, and world-class museums." Several permanent movie sets have been constructed in the past twenty years, including Lawrenceville's 31st Street Studios, the largest such installation within the interior of the country. Currently, ground has just been broken on a fifty-two-thousand-square-foot set of sound stages to be constructed (but where else?) on the site of the massive, defunct, rusting Carrie Blast Furnace in Rankin (though without Jennifer Beals this time). If

Hell being full, the dead now wander the earth. Still from *Night of the Living Dead*, 1968.

Hollywood has always sold myths of American ascendancy and greatness, then where better to do that than in Pittsburgh, on the ruins of those old sites? The 31st Street Studios, it should be obvious by now, is also housed within the complex of a former steel mill. Like the undead, Pittsburgh keeps pushing its hands upward through the soft, black dirt of its own turned-over soil, forever being resurrected for yet another night.

Chapter 6

BLACK AND GOLD
IN BLACK AND WHITE

A little under two miles north of Penn Avenue, which functions as the de facto redline of a border between Black and White across much of the east end of Pittsburgh, there is a palatial but dilapidated Queen Anne house constructed in 1894 deep within the neighborhood of Homewood West, an area that as of the 2000 census was 98.3 percent Black, as opposed to adjoining Point Breeze, which is 70 percent White. The house at 7107 Apple Street is a tall Palladian structure, wood framed with a stone base; the large home features both a gabble and turret, the last circumnavigated by a series of windows. These windows, however, are broken, boarded up with spray paint–covered wood; the shingles hang from the gable, and the building sits forlorn with no neighbors, the plot overgrown with weeds, the hill behind it scrubby with unlandscaped trees, as nature encroaches.

Abandoned for several decades, the mansion was purchased in the 1930s by William "Woogie" Harris, one of the few Black millionaires in Pittsburgh, who'd become a wealthy man as an illicit numbers runner for the Jewish mob operating several miles to the west out of the front of the Crystal Barber Shop and Billiard Parlor on Wylie Avenue in the Hill District, a neighborhood so vibrant that the Harlem Renaissance poet Countee Cullen called it the "crossroads of the world." Part of that vibrancy was due to Harris, for though his gains were ill-gotten (at least according to the law), their deployment was intended for community uplift. Harris's Homewood estate was transformed by its owner into the Mystery House, an institution that boarded Black celebrities on their sojourns through segregated Pittsburgh

The remains of the National Negro
Opera Company in Homewood.
*Photograph by Lee Paxton, distributed under a
CC-BY 2.0 license.*

who were denied lodging at the hotels Downtown, his rooms graced by
luminaries like bandleader Cab Calloway and heavyweight champion Joe
Louis (who famously defeated Billy "the Pittsburgh Kid" Conn in thirteen
rounds the summer of 1941) or local stars such as jazz singer Lena Horne
and Pirates right-fielder Roberto Clemente.

His most important contribution at the Apple Street house was renting the
third floor of the building to New England Conservatory of Music graduate
and mezzo-soprano Mary Cardwell Dawson, born in North Carolina the
same year the Queen Anne was constructed. Dawson had arrived here to
audition for a position with the Pittsburgh Opera, which she did brilliantly
but was denied on account of her race. Like so many other Black women and
men migrating north to escape the terrors of the Jim Crow South, Dawson
discovered that cities like Pittsburgh offered a gentler form of the same
racism. And so in 1941, Harris opened the Homewood house to Dawson's
National Negro Opera Company, the first of its kind, which was later to
establish offices in Newark, Chicago and Washington, D.C., but would first
mount a production of Giuseppe Verdi's Egyptian fantasy *Aida* before an
integrated audience at Oakland's Syria Mosque music hall—appropriately
enough, behind the stone sphinxes that guarded its façade.

These some two hundred performers were lauded by the national Black
newspaper the *Pittsburgh Courier*, with reporter P.L. Prattis claiming that
the singing of soprano La Julia Rhea and the rest of the cast "might have
roused Verdi himself." In the coming decades, productions would tour in
New York and Chicago; crowds of both Black and White enjoyed Verdi's
La Traviata and *Il Trovatore*, George Bizet's *Carmen* and the opera *Ouanga!*,
about the Haitian Revolution, written by the Black composer Clarence
Cameron White. Dawson rightly burnished a reputation as a visionary
force who confronted the elitist world of high culture, challenging the

79

Above: Oakland's Syria Mosque, a 3,700-seat performance hall in the Exotic Revival style and site of National Negro Opera Company performances. The hall itself was demolished in 1991. *Photograph by Edward J. Shourek, distributed under a CC-BY 2.0 license.*

Opposite: The since-removed Stephen Foster statue on Forbes Avenue. *Wikimedia Commons, distributed under a CC-BY 2.0 license.*

White gatekeepers of classical music by demonstrating the talent of Black performers. Shortly after her death in 1962, the National Negro Opera Company folded in the absence of her energy and talents; it was a few more decades of urban "redevelopment," redlining, White flight and economic stagnation that saw entropy reclaim the Queen Anne in which Harris had once done so much for Pittsburgh.

Until the spring of 2018, in the cultural center of Oakland that's only a few miles from Homewood but, socially, exists in an entirely divergent reality, a memorial rather different from the Mystery House used to sit on Forbes Avenue, shadowed by the baroque splendor of the Carnegie Museums and the Gothic majesty of the Cathedral of Learning. For twelve decades, this plot of busy land abutting Schenley Park featured a thousand-pound, ten-foot-tall memorial to the Pittsburgh-born composer Stephen Foster, an antebellum pop musician who, though raised by a wealthy White family in Lawrenceville, aspired to be the nation's "best Ethiopian songwriter." In (to put it lightly) problematic classics like "Old Folks at Home," "Camptown Races," "Beautiful Dreamer" and "Ring de Banjo," Foster composed minstrel tunes with lyrics in a pantomime of Black dialect, this consummate northerner who only traveled south once in his life inventing a halcyon,

sylvan, pastoral, bucolic fantasy of plantation life at the exact moment that millions of people were held in brutal bondage.

Unequivocally the first genuine pop entertainer in American musical history, Foster inaugurated that long tradition of White performers filching Black culture for their own purposes, an act which the cultural historian

Eric Lott succinctly describes as "love and theft." Foster's memorial was sculpted in 1900 by an Italian artist named Giuseppe Moretti; the statue had several homes in Pittsburgh before finding itself on Forbes Avenue, only a few blocks from where Dawson's *Aida* would be staged. Charmingly, the Foster memorial was supposedly financed with pennies contributed by local schoolchildren, and appropriately, Moretti's sculpture almost had the copper patina of a penny. With significantly less charm, Moretti chose to depict Foster, standing proud and erect, taking notation as the amanuensis for his muse: a wild-eyed, grinning, banjo-picking, shoeless slave who sits at the composer's feet. As the *Pittsburgh Press* reported at the time of the statue's unveiling in 1900, the memorial depicts Foster "catching the inspiration for his melodies from the fingers of an old darkey reclining at his feet."

The first narrative is one of Black excellence, of a collaborative community effort in which Dawson and her company let flower the musical talents of performers who were otherwise shut out of official institutions, while the second is about a White musician who grew wealthy by not only appropriating Black music but also denigrating the very people from whom that music derived. It's telling that of the two sites associated with Dawson and Foster, the citizenry of Pittsburgh allowed the first to be taken over by foliage and vines while the later was put on a pedestal at the center of the city's public cultural, social and intellectual life. The contrasting accounts have the feel of a parable. Such is the memorial's ugliness that the Pittsburgh Art Commission voted unanimously to remove it in 2018, and despite a few protestations by modern admirers in the comments section of the *Pittsburgh Post-Gazette* and the *Tribune Review* (as commentators on Internet articles are apt to do), the majority of Pittsburghers reacted with a collective shrug, unlike in many southern cities where similar removals have been met with opposition. The always trenchant Damon Young described the Foster memorial as the "most racist statue in America," but now the composer is being sent to Los Angeles, where he will join similar statuary as part of a modern art exhibition about how and why we choose to memorialize whom we do. As Foster comes down, meanwhile, 7107 Apple Street is restored, thanks to the indefatigable advocacy of local businesswoman Jonette Solomon, who purchased Harris's former house and has secured millions in funding to transform the former National Negro Opera Company into a museum and cultural center. This is part of a long reckoning in both U.S. and Pittsburgh history, as Harris's house is joined by institutions like the gorgeous modernist museum and performance space

The August Wilson Cultural Center. *Photograph by Minnaert, distributed under a CC-BY 2.0 license.*

named the August Wilson Cultural Center, which is directly in the heart of Downtown and dedicated to celebrating the city's greatest writer.

There are, to be sure, welcome changes that are hopefully coming to American life, but they require not only properly honoring those who came before but also ensuring that our present is as just, equitable and free for everyone, and on that latter score, we continue to fail spectacularly. The city that inculcated brilliant Black writers like Wilson and John Edgar Wideman has been graced with a resurgence of Black literary talent in the contemporary moment, authors like Brian Broome, Damon Young and Deesha Philyaw, as well as the longtime columnist and essayist Tony Norman, all probing the complexities of race, class and gender in present-day Pittsburgh. But even if prejudice isn't as obvious as when the Pittsburgh Opera—now a primary supporter of the NNOC restoration project—rejected Dawson, that doesn't mean that the city is anywhere near equally welcoming to the quarter of her citizens who are Black. Philyaw, a native of Jacksonville, made Pittsburgh her home for twenty-five years and wrote her brilliant collection *The Secret Lives of Church Ladies* here, but as she explains in a column for *Bloomberg News* in 2021, "It's time for me to leave Pittsburgh. And it's not because of the weather."

Describing how she raised her daughters here and developed a circle of literary friends, Philyaw nonetheless pointedly explains how studies have demonstrated that poverty rates and unemployment numbers for Black Pittsburghers, and specifically Black women, are worse here than in almost every other major city of comparable size. When it comes to education, health and economics, in 2021 Pittsburgh was among the bottom in terms of outcomes for its Black citizens. Citing not just its history of segregation and White flight but also the continued presence of such things, Philyaw enumerates the decimation of Black communities because of policy and structurally racist urban development schemes and the ways in which the populations of Black communities in Pittsburgh continue to decline. Comparing Pittsburgh to cities like Baltimore, Detroit and Atlanta that have fostered not just a dynamic Black cultural scene but a firm Black middle class as well, Philyaw rightly casts her eye askance at the civic boosterism of Pittsburgh leaders who trumpet claims in the national media that the city is among the most livable in the United States, asking who exactly it's livable for. As she notes, for Black residents, an accurate reading of the research rather "confirmed not only what we already know, but what we feel: Pittsburgh is not for us."

For White Pittsburghers, especially those who understand themselves to be liberal, Philyaw's column may have engendered some defensive feelings,

Pittsburgh Courier photographer Charles "Teenie" Harris—brother of Woogie—captured Pittsburgh Black life in the Hill District, such as this photo of crowds in front of the WHOD Radio Station. *Courtesy of the Carnegie Museum of Art.*

which is all the more reason to really listen to what she's saying. Foster's statue may have come down, Dawson's house may be going back up, Wilson's Hill District home is now a museum and the Carnegie Museum of Art may have a gallery dedicated to the genius photographer Charles "Teenie" Harris (brother of Woogie), but all the cultural programing and documentaries, exhibitions and monographs can't compensate for the deep inequities that are still riven in the border between Black and White in America's "Most Livable City." Drive down Fifth or Centre from the gleaming glass-and-steel skyscrapers of Downtown to the magisterial limestone buildings of Oakland and you'll pass through miles of the Hill, decimated by the "urban renewal" of the 1950s and '60s when one of America's great Black neighborhoods was destroyed by the ill-conceived plan to construct the (since demolished) Civic Arena, originally intended for musical performances but then the home for the Pittsburgh Penguins hockey team, playing, ironically, the Whitest of major league sports. Over eight thousands residents were displaced, mostly to neighborhoods like East Liberty and Homewood, while some four hundred businesses and civic institutions—jazz clubs, barbershops, restaurants, churches—were shuttered, all while traffic was redesigned to sever much of the Hill from its connections to business centers Downtown.

Marc Whittaker in *Smoketown: The Untold Story of the Other Great Black Renaissance* explains how Hill District clubs and dance halls like the Savoy, the Pythian Temple, the Bambola Social Club, Birdie Dunlap's Hurricane Club, the Collins Inn and, most of all, the Crawford Grille "produced musicians who had started to rewrite the language of jazz." This was where traveling musicians like Charles Mingus, Miles Davis and Max Roach would perform but also where homegrown talent like Earl Hines, Errol Garner, Art Blakey, Stanley Turrentine, Billy Eckstine, Lena Horne, Mary Lou Williams, George Benson, Ahmad Jamal and especially Duke Ellington's collaborator Billy Strayhorn gave Pittsburgh a music scene surpassing New York and Chicago. By 1968, following the race riots that occurred after the assassination of Martin Luther King, the Hill was left to complete decline, ignored by the White politicians who governed only a few blocks away on Downtown's Grant Street, an entire chapter of Pittsburgh's history erased and forgotten. Now the formerly dense streets of the Hill packed with rowhouses and apartments, neon jazz clubs and dynamic social halls, are replaced with overgrown empty lots, dilapidated homes and abandoned buildings, potholed streets and litter-strewn hillsides, the onetime center of the world now treated by the city as an irredeemable ghetto, a vibrant quarter made wasteland for an ice hockey team.

Duke Ellington at the piano as photographed by Harris. His Pittsburgh-born collaborator Billy Strayhorn stands to the right. *Courtesy of the Carnegie Museum of Art.*

Once there was drummer and bandleader Art Blakey with the Jazz Messengers, the incomparable cool of "Moanin'" with its initial faux-modest piano doodling and its unforgettable riff, the blast of improvisational trumpet, all of it the essence of hip. His group played hard bop, but they also knew how to swing, Blakey's Jazz Messengers formulating the postwar American avant-garde at Wylie and Centre. Pianist and composer Ahmad Jamal—a former student of Dawson—who with effortless grace swooned on "For All We Know" or who performed an electric, funky, experimental musical encomium to his hometown on the 1989 album *Pittsburgh*, was quoted by biographer Gerald Early as saying, "Pittsburgh meant everything to me and still does." There was the incomparable prodigy Mary Lou Williams, whose students included Thelonious Monk, Charlie Parker, Miles Davis and Dizzy Gillespie; her track "It Ain't Necessarily So" was the quintessence of American jazz in the postwar years. And there was velvet-voiced vocalist Lena Horne, her delivery dignified on tracks like "More Than You Know" and heartbreaking on "Sometimes I Feel Like a Motherless Child," both registers she used to effect when addressing King's March on Washington.

Then there was Horne's great friend and lifelong platonic love, Pittsburgh's Mozart Billy Strayhorn, arranger to Ellington and composer in his own right, whose "Lush Life" and "Satin Doll," among others, are as integral to anything in the American canon—not to mention "Take the A Train." All these figures, it must be emphasized, are but a small segment of the jazz luminaries educated in music programs at Westinghouse, Peabody and Schenley high schools but raised in the clubs of the Hill. Not many Pittsburghers know that the city is, appropriately, home to the International Academy of Jazz Hall of Fame, due to the efforts of Professor Nate Davis, who helped make the Music Department at the University of Pittsburgh a respected center for jazz studies, but the entirety of space devoted to the memorials are a few plaques in the William Penn Student Union where bored undergraduates drink Starbucks and eat Chipotle. Yet a few miles down Centre, Motor Square Garden's majestic topaz-blue dome rises over East Liberty, a perfect home for a museum dedicated to the jazz hall of fame, even while the space is wasted on an AAA and UPMC office. As Foster comes down, where is an equivalent monument to our jazz musicians?

The Hill District in the process of being demolished in 1969. *Photograph by Charles Harris, courtesy of the Carnegie Museum of Art.*

Black Pittsburgh's major monument is entirely more ethereal and, as a result, more permanent than bronze. Not featured in either the Schenley Plaza or the lobby of the William Penn Union, the dramatic oeuvre of August Wilson is a memorial performed onstage at the Yale Rep and Chi-Town's Goodman Theater, the Eugene O'Neill Theater in Connecticut and the Huntington in Boston, at London's Young Vic and the Pittsburgh Public Theater, in the arts center named for him Downtown and the Broadway theater dedicated to him. Nothing, in its sweep, audacity and grandeur, is quite like Wilson's *Pittsburgh Cycle*, ten plays for each of the decades of the twentieth century charting the pain and oppression, the triumph and glory, the personal and the universal of the American Black experience, with nine of those plays set in the Hill District—works like *Fences, Jitney, Gem of the Ocean, The Piano Lesson* and *Joe Turner's Come and Gone*, which transformed the narrow streets of Pittsburgh into someplace mythic, a literary imagining conjured again and again on the stages of New York and London. Characters like the 285-year-old formerly enslaved Aunt Ester, jitney manager Jim Becker, blues prodigy Floyd "Schoolboy Barton" and the rageful, prideful, hurtful and tragic former Negro League ballplayer turned garbageman Troy Maxon and his wife, Rose, who suffers all the pains and indignities of and from her husband sevenfold. "I took all my feelings, my wants and needs, my dreams…and I buried them inside you," Rose says to Troy in *Fences*, but over the years, she would "find out the soil was hard and rocky and it wasn't never gonna bloom." Such are American dreams. Unparalleled in American letters in terms of its expanse, the *Pittsburgh Cycle* is every bit as integral to American civilization as the steel we manufactured. Yet Wilson himself, fully of the Hill District but for most of his life not actually in it, was ambivalent about Pittsburgh for much the same reason later generations of Black creatives would be. "Pittsburgh is a very hard city," Wilson told an interviewer, "especially if you're black." Frequently, that's a fact that three quarters of the city would prefer not to grapple with.

White Pittsburghers, and I speak as one from birth, have a tendency to memorialize our past in terms of gentle nostalgia, a lotus-flavored miasma of platitudinous and flattering fantasies where every man is hardworking, every woman is tough but gentle, all congregations are faithful and the halupki and kielbasa are always kept warm should a cousin drop by. Only a few klicks above the Mason-Dixon Line, Pittsburgh was on the frontline of the Civil War, a steadfast Unionist city that was also a center of abolitionist thought, a sanctuary for the enslaved and their children, like the father of Black

August Wilson's childhood home in 2007, since converted into a museum and performance space. *Wikimedia Commons, distributed under a CC-BY 2.0 license.*

nationalism Martin Delaney, who found a home on its steep streets and helped establish the Hill District as "Little Haiti" in the early nineteenth century. Yet simply being on the right side of that dividing line did little to ensure that Pittsburgh wouldn't ultimately be a segregated city and a racist one (not that those two things can be extricated), for though Jim Crow wouldn't legally exist in the North, it certainly effectively did. Just being less openly racist than Birmingham or Montgomery should not have been the goal. And so, when we remember Pittsburgh history in sepia-toned imagery and jovial voice-over, we occlude how Black migrants from the South, who arrived at the same time as immigrants from southern and eastern Europe, were denied employment at the mills and membership in labor unions.

There may be gauzy Kennywood recollections of ethnic festivals and celebrations held beneath the shadow of roller coasters, but that the amusement park's pool and dance hall were steadfastly segregated until the owners were sued in 1956, at which point they simply closed the pool down, is little known by White Pittsburghers. Isaly's, a chain of restaurants famous for their chip-chopped ham barbecue sandwiches and skyscraper ice cream cones (as well as being the birthplace of the Klondike Bar) refused to seat Black customers at their lunch counters well into the civil rights era. The thriving underground business of unlicensed jitneys, from which Wilson drew the name for his titular play, existed only because yellow cabs refused to pick up Black passengers. Were this legacy of racism not baked into the economic, social and cultural structures of urban life, it would be more forgivable that there is little discussion of it, yet after examining contemporary racialized disparities in poverty, healthcare and education, University of Pittsburgh law professor Jerry Dickinson concluded in a 2021 essay for *Public Source* that "Pittsburgh is not the nation's most livable city. It is America's apartheid city."

Mass disenfranchisement is grotesque enough, but the ironic tragedy of Pittsburgh's racial stratification is that so much of what's built at the expense

Charles Harris photograph of Doris Clark on Buick, with steel mill in the background, 1945. *Courtesy of the Carnegie Museum of Art.*

of its Black citizens also serves to entomb the rich cultural legacy of Black Pittsburghers' contributions. Dawson is a case in point, as are the clubs of Wylie and Centre Avenue that acted as a jazz academy for decades of the twentieth century. So crucial was the Hill District to the development of modern American culture that Whittaker claims the neighborhood was a "black version of the story of fifteenth-century Florence and early twentieth-century Vienna: a miraculous flowering of social and cultural achievement all at once, in one small city" (I've quoted that same passage in *An Alternative History of Pittsburgh* precisely because I think it's so important to keep foregrounded). Today, by contrast, many White Pittsburghers only celebrate the achievements of Black Pittsburghers if they're accomplished on the gridiron of Heinz Field, and that can be very much contingent on whether the Steelers are winning or not (don't see what they say about Coach Mike Tomlin in the comments section). It's currently politically fashionable among some to pretend that we need only remember history though a maudlin lens of innocence, that to be too critical of that which we deserve to be critical of is somehow a disservice to the present, though the self-evident foolishness of such reasoning barely needs to be commented on.

What does matter are the harsh details of the past, for the Hill District's renaissance existed during the lifetime of people who are able to read this book, and the policies that led to its destruction were promulgated during living memory as well. Politics and economics conspired to demolish the Hill, so that even after thousands of its residents were displaced to neighborhoods such as East Liberty, that later area would also see itself separated from the rest of the city with a mutilating redirect of traffic designed by urban planners at Carnegie Tech, a once-prosperous area similarly transformed by quasi-intentional blight. Now that East Liberty—the neighborhood in which I spent my first few years of life and where I attended middle school—has seen a resurgence of economic development, including the construction of office buildings, hotels, restaurants and shops, as well as the location of corporate offices for tech giants like Google and Duolingo, there is a discussion that needs to be had about the ways in which gentrification contributes to racial stratification in Pittsburgh, with longtime residents priced out of their homes as areas become more fashionable (according to the National Community Reinvestment Corporation, the city is the eighth most gentrified in the United States, surpassing even San Francisco). "This is business," says a character in Wilson's final play *Radio Golf*. "This is the way it's done in America." When it comes to the vagaries of race and development in America, it's ever been such. As the backdrop to *Radio Golf*, Wilson imagined the possibility of Pittsburgh electing its first Black mayor in 2005. It wouldn't actually happen for another seventeen years.

Chapter 7

THE PITTSBURGH SCHOOL

You can't think small in a steel mill.
—*Jack Gilbert in the* Paris Review *(2005)*

And there were so many Pittsburgh poets in my hallway that if, at that instant,
a meteorite had come smashing through my roof, there would never have been
another stanza written about rusting fathers and impotent steelworks
and the Bessemer converter of love.
—*Michael Chabon,* Wonder Boys *(1995)*

Editor John Scull's printshop was only a few hundred yards from Market Square, where two-storied buildings were just beginning to rise along the perimeter, some constructed from the timber and brick pulled from the walls of Fort Pitt's ruins after it was abandoned by the newly constituted Army of the United States of America in 1792. Scull had arrived in the settlement of some thousand people in 1786, when "Pittsburgh" was still pronounced in the Scottish manner rather than in the German form. The United States was only a decade old. Before it was America, Pittsburgh was in Great Britain, mostly in the colony of Pennsylvania but briefly as part of Virginia. This area was part of New France for longer than it was ever British, though for most of its history, the region was part of the Iroquois Confederacy (it still is). Like most citizens in the nascent city, Scull was not originally a Pittsburgher, having been born hundreds of miles to the east in the far larger community of Reading. Having attempted to make his career in Philadelphia, Scull decided like many others that his fortunes would be in the West. Having hauled type keys, ink and paper over the commonwealth's mountainous divide, starting in the summer of 1786, Scull's press would produce a four-page edition of the *Pittsburgh Gazette* every week, the first such publication west of the Alleghenies. Edward Park Anderson, writing in a 1931 issue of the journal *Western Pennsylvania History*, explains that in addition to news from Philadelphia and London, New York and Boston, the *Pittsburgh Gazette* also printed "local writers, who with little originality, discussed the wisdom of remaining a bachelor, the wickedness of gaming, and the virtue of women." Scull, as the primary editor and the only printer in the city, was library, archive and salon in one simple shop. Such was the literary culture of Pittsburgh, as it existed at the time.

The two centuries hence have been more fruitful, even if national critics don't ascribe to the Three Rivers the same literary significance that they would to the cities of the East Coast or, later, the West Coast. New York had Henry James and Edith Wharton, Boston was home to Nathaniel Hawthorne and Louisa May Alcott and urban latecomer Chicago can boast Carl Sandburg and Saul Bellow. Los Angeles may have given the world noir with Raymond Chandler and Dashiell Hammett, but when it comes to a distinctive "Pittsburgh School" of literature, such a designation seems not just a misnomer but something not even considered. This is not for lack of talent—Pittsburgh has produced or strongly influenced Willa Cather, Gertrude Stein, Thomas Bell, Rachel Carson, Kenneth Burke, James Laughlin, Robinson Jeffers, Malcolm Cowley, Edward Abbey, W.D. Snodgrass, John Edgar Wideman, Annie Dillard, Michael Chabon, Stewart O'Nan and Terrence Hayes, which isn't even to begin grappling with the imposing theatrical monument that is August Wilson's unparalleled *Pittsburgh Cycle* or contemporary prodigies like Brian Broome, Deesha Philyaw, Brian Bacharach, Ellen Litman and Damon Young. Even our two Saint Andys— Carnegie and Warhol—produced prose in the form of *The Gospel of Wealth* and *The Philosophy of Andy Warhol (From A to B & Back Again)*, which have their own unusual charms. Like Ireland or Czechoslovakia, Pittsburgh has produced literary wealth far beyond its relative size. Nobody less than Herman Melville would write in 1850 that "men not very much inferior to Shakespeare are this day being born on the banks of the Ohio," but the establishment of anything that could be considered a cohesive "Pittsburgh School," something that unites Cathar with Hayes, Carson with Bell, remains elusive. An oversight, because I'd argue that any consideration of the canon of Pittsburgh easily demonstrates a unifying thread, as diverse as the writers

Left: Willa Cather in 1920. *Wikimedia Commons, distributed under a CC-BY 2.0 license.*

Right: Gertrude Stein in 1935. *Photograph by Carl van Vechten, distributed under a CC-BY 2.0 license.*

from this city have been, which connects all the way from Scull's workshop to today's Madwoman in the Attic workshops hosted by Carlow University or the readings at Bloomfield's White Whale Bookstore.

The land of the Ohio confluence is defined by geographical liminality: neither east nor west and strung along the border between south and north. The original major metropolis was established *after* the United States itself, so that Pittsburgh was the first new place, the oldest new place. Unlike Boston, New York or Philadelphia, Pittsburgh was really built as an American city and not as a European city in exile. The result is that of urban literatures, Pittsburgh's was the first to grapple with what the word *American* meant, and its in-between position within the country allowed itself to continue doing so over the next two centuries. If it's been difficult to parse out a separate Pittsburgh School, then arguably it's because the writing of the city is as synonymous with America as the city is with the nation. The writers of Pittsburgh were the first not to look toward the Atlantic and Europe but rather toward the continent and beyond, in a literature that progresses westward with the course of empire and all the brutal settler-colonialism and then industrial capitalism that would follow. That most of those with quill in hand wrote forgettable doggerel and essays about women's chastity during the days when Fort Pitt was being disassembled doesn't mean that all of them lacked vision, however.

On Market Street in the eighteenth century, an ink-stained Scull with calloused hands laboriously placed lead and tin key types into the press, where he would have heard haggling over produce and meat in the square's stalls and the hawking of tinkers selling domestic wares on their way into the Ohio Territory, the brawling of drunken soldiers in the taverns, the clang of iron in blacksmith forges and the barking of dogs and squealing of pigs in the yards of his neighbors. Across the Monongahela, he would have seen miners cutting into the steep mountainside known as Coal Hill but soon to be named after the first president, the burning of this fuel coating the buildings of Pittsburgh in an eye-stinging grime and soot, the miasma of particulate mingling with the odor of offal and the smell of shit (horse and human): a pastoral land already smudged on its forehead with the mark of industry, what poet Jack Gilbert would call two centuries later a "tough heaven."

Bundled and distributed to subscribers, the *Pittsburgh Gazette* carried news of the Constitution's ratification (among the first papers to print it in its entirety), of the nearby Whiskey Rebellion in 1791 and of Meriweather Lewis and William Clark's 1803 departure from the confluence of the Ohio to points farther West. Something far more remarkable, however, than a mere newspaper, came off Scull's press in 1792. That was the year that Scull would publish a volume penned by his fellow easterner, business partner and cofounder of the newspaper—the first edition in an ongoing serial publication by Scotsman and lawyer Hugh Henry Brackenridge titled *Modern Chivalry: Containing the Adventures of Captain John Farrago and Teague O'Regan, His Servant*. Like Lewis and Clark, Farrago does "ride about the world a little, with his man Teague at his heels, to see how things were going on here and there, and to observe human nature." Brackenridge's *Modern Chivalry* would be the first novel written and published in Pittsburgh. Even more remarkable, and contrary to Anderson's contention that during the eighteenth century "Pittsburgh developed no culture of its own," *Modern Chivalry* would also be the first novel published in the new republic of the United States. American literature was born in Pittsburgh.

To argue what the first *American* literature is remains largely an issue of semantics, of considering what regions, languages and peoples have produced such a literature, with courses in early American writing including the usual suspects like John Winthrop's Puritan sermon "A Model of Christian Charity" and Benjamin Franklin's thrifty autobiography and more nebulous entries based on broad New World thematic concerns, allowing Thomas More's

Utopia and William Shakespeare's *The Tempest* to, rather creatively, be classified as part of our national cannon. As interesting as those debates are at the level of theory, Brackenridge's novel is something different, a child of convenience that emerges from the definitive 1776 date of the United States' creation—the first novel published in the new nation, as definitive a fact as can be established. The first instalment of *Modern Chivalry* predates by six years the 1798 Gothic novel *Wieland; or the Transformation* by Brackenridge's fellow Pennsylvanian the Philadelphian Charles Brockden Brown, which is frequently configured as the "first" novel in the new United States.

Hugh Henry Brackenridge.

Etching of Hugh Henry Brackenridge, author of *Modern Chivalry*. *Wikimedia Commons, distributed under a CC-BY 2.0 license.*

Pittsburgh, so often ignored by our eastern cousins, was denied the auspicious honor of the first novel in the new country from the very beginning, passed over in Philadelphia, New York and Boston before Brackenridge's novel was yet sold. Yet while Brockden Brown's Gothic tales feel positively European, Brackenridge's backcountry epic is a novel equivalent with the frontier. *Modern Chivalry*, despite borrowing from European forms, is consummately American, especially as regarding our own democratic ambivalences, with Philip Gura in *Truth's Ragged Edge: The Rise of the American Novel* explaining how this narrative that takes place in Western Pennsylvania in the years after the Whiskey Rebellion is a "loose and baggy picaresque…that through satire probe[s] the country's new social order, in particular the still-uncomfortable notion that the most plebian citizen should be afforded the same respect as a person of wealth and influence." The United States of America, formed through the writing act itself and willed into reality through the force of an idea rather than anything else, is a uniquely literary nation, the "greatest of poems" as Walt Whitman had it. American literature is distinguished by being obsessed with defining what exactly America is (in the same way that all poetry is really about poetry) because this is a covenantal nation far more than it is a mere assemblage of people. In that way, *Modern Chivalry* is the first of this type. Farrago and Teague setting out on the road are Huck and Finn; they are Dean Moriarty and Sal Paradise. The subject remains the same—America.

An 1882 illustration of the Whiskey Rebellion that occurred between 1791 and 1794.
Those events are a key part of *Modern Chivalry*'s narrative. *Wikimedia Commons, distributed under
a CC-BY 2.0 license.*

Farrago, like his creator, is a man of contradictions: unabashedly
elitist, dismissive of the poor and unlearned who compose the bulk of the
settlement's populace and yet contemptuous of the wealthy and powerful.
The novel embodies the ambivalences of an author once a Federalist and
then a Jeffersonian, equally of the East and of the West. Across eight
hundred sprawling pages, *Modern Chivalry* recounts the travels of aristocratic
and rational Farrago, the Don Quixote of the tale, with his Sancho Panza in
the form of comedic and foolish Teague (a Scotts Presbyterian, Brackenridge
is as generous in his depiction of the Irish Catholic O'Regan as can be
expected). Doing in fiction what De Tocqueville would accomplish with his
travelogue *Democracy in America* some years later, *Modern Chivalry* episodically
recounts Farrago and O'Regan's interactions with the commonfolk between
Philadelphia and Pittsburgh. Brackenridge's characteristic border-country
skepticism of central authority—so Scottish and Appalachian—is obvious
in the novel. "You have nothing but your character, Teague, in a new
country to depend on," Farrago says to his manservant after the latter is
somehow elected to Congress. "Let it never be said, that you quitted an
honest livelihood, the taking care of my horse, to follow the newfangled
whims of the time, and to be a statesman." Class divisions, ever an American
problem, ever a Pittsburgh one, were visible to anxious Brackenridge, who
despite being a gentleman lived not more than a minute from the city's
poorest inhabitants in a settlement so small. The author's sentiments were
often as contradictory as Farrago's were, with Cathy Davidson writing in
Revolution and the Word: The Rise of the Novel in America that Brackenridge was a
"curious combination of elitist and plebian, of Princeton-educated classicist

and backwoods lawyer," a man who "frequently appeared in court rumpled and dirty, his hair unkempt, without socks, and, more than once, without shoes." This was a gentleman who not only wrote the first American novel and cofounded the city's first newspaper but also established the institution that would one day grow into the University of Pittsburgh. Brackenridge, the lawyer who during a rainstorm wished to avoid getting the single suit he owned wet so he elected to ride his horse through Pittsburgh in the nude, because "the storm, you know, would spoil the clothes, but it couldn't spoil me." If Pittsburgh writers are anything, it's against pretension.

Imagining Brackenridge as the spiritual godfather of the literature of the United States is perhaps an issue of simple chronology, but to posit him as a uniquely Pittsburgh author is arguably more critical conceit than demonstrable reality. Categorizing *Modern Chivalry* as proletarian literature would be fallacious, though Brackenridge did have opprobrium "reserved for rich land speculators who…exploited the penury of others and profited at the expense of the whole nation," as Davidson writes. This was combined with the skeptical wisdom wherein Brackenridge holds that the "demagogue is the first great destroyer of the constitution by deceiving the people. He is no democrat that deceiveth the people. He is an aristocrat." Anti-pretension is maybe just the softer form of the radical qualities we associate with the proletarian novel, and the Pittsburgh School has, as material conditions necessitate within the industrial city, always had an intimate relationship to the physicality of work and an allergy to unearned ethereality. This is, after all, a hard paradise of kiln and forge, mill and factory.

Still, I'd argue that all the major concerns of *Modern Chivalry*'s creator are explicit in the school that would come to develop afterward, even if Wilson and Dillard weren't sitting with copies of that eighteenth-century novel open in front of them. What Brackenridge, Wilson, Dillard and every other potential member of the Pittsburgh School happen to share is a concern with materiality and with the sublime attributes of landscape and the industrial labor that was facilitated by that landscape. Furthermore, and in the truest honor of those conflicted and conflicting subjects, such writing is always about America, since anything that fully expresses Pittsburgh must also completely interrogate the nation of which it is a part. The United States of Ambivalence, a nation both Eden and Babylon, Genesis and Armageddon, supposedly of unlimited promise but also defined by the filthy and cruel manner in which said promise is fulfilled. "Nature is here in her bloom; no decay or decrepitude," wrote Brackenridge, considering the mountain streams flowing into the Monongahela and the Allegheny, the verdant spring

Scottish-born Pittsburgh painter John Kane's *The Monongahela River Valley, Pennsylvania*, 1931. *Image courtesy of the Metropolitan Museum of Art, New York.*

along the Appalachians. "All fragrancy, health, and vivacity," but Paradise still remains workable land, after all. Brackenridge writes that the men of Pittsburgh must be workers in "iron and in leather, and in wood. Invention, as well as industry, must be requisite." And so it was.

Thomas Bell's (née Adalbert Thomas Belejcak) proletarian masterpiece, the 1941 novel *Out of This Furnace: A Novel of Immigrant Labor*, bears little similarity at the surface level to *Modern Chivalry*—the latter with its chauvinistic extolling of Anglo-Saxon values as pioneers set out on the Western frontier and the former about the experience of degradation, exploitation and poverty among the immigrants who worked in steel mills owned and operated by the proverbial great-great-grandchildren of a man like Brackenridge—yet both books share the Pittsburgh School's perseveration on industry and physicality, with the paradox of finding a heaven in a hell. A sprawling family epic, *Out of This Furnace* begins with the arrival of Slovakian immigrant Djuro Kracha in Braddock, where he works at the (still extant) Edgar Thomson Steelworks. The narrative follows his daughter Mary and her husband, Mike Dobrejcak, who also labors within the mills, and finally concludes with the

The Edgar Thomson
Works in the mid-
1990s. *Photograph
by David Rochberg,
distributed under a CC-
BY 2.0 license.*

third generation, when their son Dobie Dobrejcak agitates on behalf of a
successful union organization effort. Evoking the great working-class novels
of the first half of the twentieth century, such as Tillie Olsen's 1930s *Yonnondio:
From the Thirties* and Pietro Di Donato's 1939 *Christ in Concrete*, Bell's novel
is concerned with the "acculturation and evolving political consciousness
of the immigrant workers of America's steel towns," as David Demarest
matter-of-factly explains in his afterword to the 1976 reprint. Bell bluntly
stated in a 1946 interview with the ethnic Lemka newspaper *Ludovy dennik*
that "I saw a people brought here by steel magnates from the old country
and exploited, ridiculed, and oppressed," and indeed the novel itself is in
part a defense of the maligned "mill hunkie," the eastern European laboring
class that constituted the bulk of workers during these decades.

Only a few miles to the east of Pittsburgh, Braddock is a representative
Western Pennsylvania mill town: the hulking golem of the Edgar Thomson
Steel Works rusting by the banks of the Monongahela, hundreds of thousands
of immigrant men laboring on behalf of first Carnegie Steel and then U.S.
Steel in unimaginably dangerous conditions. Braddock, Pennsylvania, is the
literal setting of *Out From This Furnace*, but as Bell well knew, there were many
Braddocks—in Connellsville and Homestead, McKeesport and Tarentum.
In Pittsburgh, too. Working in a mill, especially in the decades before
widespread labor organization ensured a basic degree of safety precautions,
which were further strengthened by federal regulations, was a dangerous
means of employment. Men frequently incurred horrible injuries at places
like Edgar Thomson, Homestead Steel Works or Jones and Laughlin. Men
died from exposure, from being crushed, by being burned. This isn't even to
consider the sorts of ways that such physical labor can break down the body

Molten pig iron being poured at the Jones and Loughlin plant on the South Side in 1942. Note the comparatively small size of the worker to the left. *Photograph by U.S. Office of War Information, distributed under a CC-BY 2.0 license.*

itself over the course of decades: the strained muscles and calloused flesh, the sprained backs and slipped discs. *Out From This Furnace* concerns itself with physicality in this intimate sort of way; it's materialist in its broadly Marxian politics, but more than as a method of analysis, matter is the realm in which his characters are forced to operate, the undeniable reality of not just capital and labor but of molten steel as well (and what that liquid metal can do to a human body).

Yet part of what defines the Pittsburgh School, from Brackenridge onward, is the mystical kernel of something beyond mere matter that animates any consideration of this place: the transcendent in the prosaic, the sacred in the profane. An intimation of beauty amid a kingdom of ugliness. "Looking up," Bell writes, one can see the "furnaces and stoves, piled one behind the other into the distance, small lights, and over beyond the rail mill the wavering glow of the Bessemers. A steel mill at night made a man feel small as he trudged into its pile of structures, its shadows." Certainly Pittsburgh literature isn't the only body of writing that can examine the cracked beauty of the rusted, hulking material world, of the utopian hid within the grimiest of places, but it's the overwhelming obsession of all prose and poetry that is indelibly marked by the Steel City, the wisdom that comes from the sublimity of industry. "A cast-house filled…with illumination as the furnace was tapped and the bright glare of the molten metal was like a conflagration around the end of an alleyway, silhouetting waiting ladles, the corner of an engine house, skeleton beams."

Bell's grandparents came to America from Slovakia, but the ancestors of John Edgar Wideman arrived in America on a very different boat, and that, as is always the case in America, makes an important difference. He was descended from enslaved African Americans on both sides of his family—his mother's people were from Maryland and his father's from South Carolina—and the family was part of the Great Migration northward from the states of the former Confederacy to cities like Pittsburgh. If Wilson had the Hill, then Wideman has Homewood, his trilogy of books about that Black neighborhood in Pittsburgh's east end describes a community as evocative as James Joyce's Dublin or William Faulkner's Yoknapatawpha County. Wideman's prodigious literary output is strongly marked by the difficult contradictions of American life; he is the Rhodes Scholar who attended the University of Pennsylvania on an academic scholarship, was foundational in the creation of African American studies as a discipline at his alma mater and was a two-time winner of the PEN/Faulkner Award, while his brother and son were both convicted in two separate murder trials. In experimental, incandescent prose across novels, short stories and memoir, Wideman explores these contingencies of race and trauma in works like *The Lynchers, Reuben, Philadelphia Fire, The Cattle Killing, Two Cities* and *Brothers and Keepers*, but it is arguably the Homewood Trilogy for which he will be most valorized. Though Wideman's novels range over the globe, across America, Europe and Africa, it is the working-class Black neighborhood of his youth that provides a geography of the soul. Even though the narratively interconnected works were never intended to be written as a trilogy, the 1981 short story collection *Damballah*, the novel *Hiding Place* from that same year and the novel *Sent For You Yesterday* from 1983, have been published as an omnibus since 1985, editors seeing the subconscious connections that aren't always intentional. What Wideman presents in these three works is an alternate mythogeography of the American experience relying on the aesthetics of the author's home city in its expression of the paradoxes of beauty and ugliness that define existence in Pittsburgh.

As a series of short stories, *Damballah*—named after the serpentine demiurge who creates the world in the complex mythological system of West African and Caribbean Voudon—presents an alternate history of Homewood, Pittsburgh and the United States, for as Walton Muyumba writes in his foreword to the career-spanning collection *You Made Me Love You: Selected Stories, 1981–2018*, "Wideman's art is rooted in Homewood's idiom thus; it rises from the blues aesthetic tradition and speaks universally," rhetorically placing the author in a lineage of Pittsburgh jazz musicians that includes Billy Strayhorn, Mary Lou Williams, Art Blakey, Ahmad Jamal and Billy Eckstine. Like a jazz musician improvising a theme, *Damballah* draws from both invention and family folklore, crafting a creation myth for the neighborhood. Presented as a letter between an unnamed narrator writing on an idyllic Greek isle to his brother in prison, Wideman's story claims that Homewood was founded the year before Fort Sumter by their great-great-great-grandmother, the oracularly named Sybil Owens, who escaped from slavery in Cumberland, Maryland. "I heard her laugher, her amens, and can I get a witness, her digressions, the web she spins and brushes away with her hands," writes Wideman. "What seems to ramble begins to cohere when the listener understands the process, understands the voice seeks to recover everything, that the voice proclaims nothing is lost," or as one of the author's favorite aphorisms has it, "All stories are true." As is the nature, purpose and utility of creation myths, Wideman's story "The Beginning of Homewood" shouldn't be read as a literal or historical account of the neighborhood's origins but rather as a riff on how we generate meaning out of the stories we tell. History, as a nightmare to which we're ever waking, can't quite be escaped in Wideman's works, but there can be shards of luminescence despite the darkness. Homewood, in the author's descriptions, is a tough place, an ugly place. "Somebody should make a deep ditch out of Homewood Avenue…and just go and push the rowhouses and boarded storefronts into the hole. Bury it all." And yet, as is ever true of the metaphysics of the Pittsburgh School, there is a temporary utopia oft in the moment, where even the names of "streets can open like the gates of a great city, everyone who's ever inhabited that city, walked its streets, suddenly, like a shimmer, like the first notes of a Monk solo, breathing, moving, a world quickens as the gates swing apart."

By distance, Annie Dillard's Pittsburgh was preposterously close to that of Wideman's, the neighborhoods of the former's wealthy Point Breeze and the latter's impoverished Homewood separated by only a few blocks, Penn Avenue functioning as a spiritual boundary between the two. On one side

Abandoned rowhouses in Homewood, 2011. *Image courtesy of State Senator Jay Costa.*

were ivy-covered, granite-stoned Tudor homes, on the other long lines of broken brick rowhouses. Frequently categorized as a nature writer—a not incorrect though arguably incomplete designation—Dillard is an author of lyrical nonfiction; her 1974 *Pilgrim at Tinker Creek* and 1982 *Teaching a Stone to Talk* conceive of the environment through a distinctly Christian understanding, yet she is aware that the world is always mediated through human perspective (and often human intervention). Hers is a nature that is somehow both Darwinian and endowed with meaning, where following the "one extravagant gesture of creation in the first place, the universe has continued to deal exclusively in extravagances, flinging intricacies and colossi down aeons of emptiness, heaping profusions on profligacies with ever-fresh vigor. The whole world has been on fire from the word go," as she writes in *Pilgrim at Tinker Creek*. "But everywhere I look I see fires; that which isn't flint is tinder, and the whole world sparks and flames."

Like Bell's colossal steel mill or Wideman's streets metaphorically thrumming with the sound of Thelonious Sphere Monk, Dillard's world is endowed with tongues of fire. In her 1985 memoir *An American Childhood*, Dillard refers to her childhood neighborhood as the "Valley of the Kings," comparing this abode where once Carnegie, Frick, Westinghouse and Heinz built their palatial estates to the Pharaonic Necropolis of ancient Egypt. By

Only a mile away but a universe apart from Homewood. A Point Breeze house on Reynolds Street, a block from where Annie Dillard grew up. *Photograph by Cbail19, distributed under a CC-BY 2.0 license.*

the time of her youth in the '50s, the area was solidly upper middle class (her father was an oil executive, and she attended the exclusive Ellis School), yet the remnants of its much more opulent Gilded Age past still marked Point Breeze. Evidence of the tremendous wealth that shaped the city was everywhere, in robber baron mansions subdivided into apartments and the wrought-iron gate that used to be H.J. Heinz's fence running alongside blocks of Penn Avenue only a few minutes from Wideman's Homewood. Pittsburgh was built on top of itself, its history waiting to be excavated as it were that actual Valley of the Kings. This setting helped to develop Dillard's gift for sensory detail, which she has honed into an almost theological precision. In her memoir, Dillard recounts how when she officially left the Presbyterian Church as an adolescent, the minister told her that she would be back, and in many ways he was correct (if not in the way he intended).

Her prose (which has more than a bit of the poetic about it) adopted the sacramental poetics of a Gerard Manley Hopkins or a William Blake with awareness that the world is simultaneously fallen and enchanted with a charged energy. As she writes, "Skin was earth; it was soil. I could see, even on my own skin, the joined trapezoids of dust specks God had wetted and stuck with his spit the morning he made Adam from dirt. Now, all these generations later, we people could still see on our skin the inherited prints of the dust specks of Eden." Within Dillard's writing, there is this perseveration on the possibility of transcendence in the mundane and the sacred in the profane, that overweening concern of the Pittsburgh School. Dillard may be most celebrated for bringing this awareness to her observations of the natural world in rural Virginia, but it was a spiritual skill inculcated by the contradictions of Pittsburgh, where rusting mills abut massive parks. That environment was her first tutor in the personal vocabulary of matter and spirit. Indeed, the first few pages of *An American Childhood* provide a sterling example of the Pittsburgh School's fascination with materiality and the way in which certain immanent enchantments can be implied by nature.

Until recently, Pittsburgh had a grim reputation in the national media, the stereotypes of the smoggy, smoky city that appeared as a "hell with the lid off," in the memorable description of the *Atlantic Monthly* correspondent James Parton in 1868. In such portrayals, the fact is often occluded that this is a place that is incandescently beautiful. The Pittsburgh School is enmeshed in the physicality of place not just because of industry but because the terrain and topography of the city is so shockingly dramatic, so astounding, so otherworldly. "When everything else has gone from my brain," writes

Nine Mile Run during winter, deep within Frick Park, which borders Point Breeze. *Photograph by Jims Maher, distributed under a CC-BY 2.0 license.*

Dillard at the beginning of *An American Childhood*, "when all this has dissolved, what will be left, I believe, is topology: the dreaming memory of land as it lay this way and that." Pittsburgh literature uses abstraction, but it is not a literature of abstraction. It is very much centered in place: in the hills, rivers, mountains and valleys, in the earth itself. From the dross material of place then comes forth the ethereality of transcendence. In Pittsburgh, abstraction is the child of the concrete and not the other way around.

"I will see the city poured rolling down the mountain valleys like slag, and see the city lights sprinkled and curved around the hills' curves, rows of bonfires winding," writes Dillard. "At sunset a red light like housefires shines from the narrow hillside windows; the houses' bricks burn like glowing coals." Note how she elevates the vocabulary of industry—slag, glowing coals—and transmutes them into the landscape; a transubstantiation of grit into gold, marked by a scriptural parallelism. "The tall buildings rise lighted to their tips. Their lights illumine other buildings' clean sides, and illumine the narrow city canyons below," as Dillard describes the totemistic beauty of the Golden Triangle, the spangled tableau that announces itself to visitors as they depart from the Fort Pitt Tunnel over Downtown Pittsburgh at the confluence of the Three Rivers. And as Dillard knows, the human creations of beauty are only ever borrowed from the earth, which is simultaneously exploited and loved by civilization but, regardless, will always be that which is victorious. "When the shining city, too, fades," in eons hence, what will remain are those "forested mountains and hills, and the way the rivers lie flat and moving, among them, and the way the low land lies wooden among them, and the blunt mountains rise in darkness from the rivers' banks, steep from the rugged south and rolling from the north."

Any good materialist knows that culture builds itself on the physical world; in the tough heaven of Pittsburgh, denial of that basic axiom is an impossibility. The poetics of Pittsburgh—if we can speak of such a thing— provide an additional gloss to that axiom in the form of the foolish wisdom that comprehends that materiality pushed to its extreme doesn't just allow for the spiritual but demands it, that sees something revolutionary in the transcendent, the ecstatic, the mystical. This is the beautiful surrealism of Michael Chabon's *The Mysteries of Pittsburgh*, where the concrete and iron power station in the ravine of Panther Hollow between the Carnegie Museum and Carnegie Mellon University is a "cloud factory," where in Pittsburgh the "sky glowed and flashed orange, off toward the mills in the south, as if volcano gods were fighting there or, it seemed to me, as if the end of the world had begun; it was an orange so tortured and final."

Pittsburgh skyline and nature, 2022. *Wikimedia Commons, distributed under a CC-BY 2.0 license.*

This, then, is the fullest summation of the Pittsburgh School's central aesthetic: not that it's concerned only with being blue collar and working class or that it's all about industry or even the landscape (though it is about all those things) but that it deigns to acknowledge the sacredness hidden within an old brick building, a rusting foundry, a litter-strewn river bank. That it's a variety of writing that fundamentally says yes to the numinous, yes to the holy, yes to the beautiful, not in spite of those things being hard to perceive but precisely because they are so often hidden. "Pittsburgh persists in being existentially itself," writes poet Samuel Hazo in his 1986 essay "The Pittsburgh That Stays Within You." "It simply but inevitably and determinedly keeps becoming what it is," and this is the subtle ingredient that defines a specific poetics of Pittsburgh.

Furthermore, this is the indelible effect that Pittsburgh has on those of us from here, especially for those of us who are only able to make sense of things through that imperfect medium of words, because as natives to this beautiful and cursed land we are never able to leave and always determined to come back. What Jan Beatty describes in her 2017 collection *Jackknife: New and Selected Poems* when she writes of being "filled with sediment: / with tough, dirty Pittsburgh / where the mountains of black rock & / half mills are carapaces" or Patricia Dobler's sense in her 1986 *Talking to Strangers* about how "the sun rose in sulphur / piercing the company house" so that our "soft bones eaten with flesh...tempered the heart of the eater." Steel City aesthetics are all about contrast or maybe, more appropriately, paradox, for it's not that the city is tough and beautiful but rather that heaven itself should look like Pittsburgh. Judith Vollmer in her 1998 *The Door Open to the Fire* looks out from Mount Washington, toward the direction where Scull once printed his newspaper, and she claims that "under fog that falls...Pittsburgh stands in for Paris, San Francisco, / even a minor, gritty Rome," while Joseph Bathanti, now the poet laureate of North Carolina but a Pittsburgher originally, writes in *Sun Magazine* that we can expect that in the hereafter "angels from the ether / bear platters of ravioli / from Groceria Italiano / in Bloomfield; sausage / from Joe Grasso on Larimer Avenue; / lemon ice from Moio's; / *sfogliatelles* from Barsotti; / Parmesan, aged for eternity."

In my experience, the only people who hate Pittsburgh are those who've never come here or those who've never left. There is a hard-worn wisdom within this terrain and in being able to compare it to elsewhere. Pittsburgh writers don't deny the materiality of our circumstances, so that when ethereality arrives, it's as a difficult grace. Tough heaven, indeed. Gerald Stern, poet laureate of New Jersey but fundamentally always of Pittsburgh, the Allderdice graduate from Squirrel Hill, writes in one of his most famous lyrics from 1984's *This Time: New and Selected Poems* about his family learning

Downtown Pittsburgh at the confluence of the three rivers. *Wikimedia Commons, distributed under a CC-BY 2.0 license.*

109

of the end of World War II in that "tiny living room / on Beechwood Boulevard." Millions of Stern's fellow Jews burned in the ovens of Hitler, so much more hideous than the furnaces of Pennsylvania, but despite such evil, the poet and his family dance joyfully at the end of the war, "my hair all streaming, / my mother red with laughter, / my father cupping / his left hand under his armpit, doing the dance / of old Ukraine." This is a wisdom that sees genesis in every apocalypse, that understands the presence of God among "wrinkled ties and baseball trophies and coffee pots." They aren't in Poland or Germany, but from five thousand miles away, the Sterns genuflect before the "God of mercy…wild God." He describes the "three of us whirling and singing, the three of us / screaming and falling…as if we could never stop," even here in the "home / of the evil Mellons," in "Pittsburgh, beautiful filthy Pittsburgh." It's a spiritual truth of the Pittsburgh School, this understanding that filth and beauty aren't in contradiction but rather they justify themselves and each other—a truth of the great patriarchs and prophets, a scriptural truth. Stern's friend Jack Gilbert, with whom he would drunkenly traipse through the streets of East Liberty, understood Pittsburgh similarly. "The rusting mills sprawled gigantically / along three rivers. The authority of them," writes Gilbert in *Tough Heaven: Poems of Pittsburgh*. The "gritty alleys where we played every evening were / stained pink by the inferno always surging in the sky, / as though Christ and the Father were still fashioning / the Earth." What Pittsburgh represents, for Gilbert, is a place embodying the principle of the "beauty forcing us as much as harshness." Here, then, are the poetics of Pittsburgh—the way the low winter light strikes gray slag along the banks of the Monongahela, a chipped plaster statue of the blue-robed Virgin Mary encircled in a buried porcelain tub on a browning Greenfield lawn, a daisy pushing through cracked Bloomfield concrete, the low glide of a peregrine falcon as it launches itself from the towers of Oakland. On earth as it is in Pittsburgh.

Chapter 8

ALLEGHENY GOTHIC

B eneath the basements of tony Lawrenceville—where the young gather on Sundays for brunch at Geppetto Café or the Abbey to cure the hangovers caught at Belvedere's or New Amsterdam the night before and where audiences enjoy craft brews while watching an art movie at Row House Cinema, perhaps after purchasing a tasteful mid-century modern sofa or chair from Pittsburgh Furniture—there is a mass grave with some five hundred anonymous bodies buried, the bulk of them children. On annexation of Lawrenceville in 1868, the city exhumed and reburied all the corpses in what was then known as the Washington Burial Ground, with the few whose bodies could be identified reinterred in the nearby, bucolic, sylvan and wholly more contemporary Allegheny Cemetery, while the unfortunate nameless were heaped into a small burial plot. Among the oldest settlements east of the Golden Triangle, Lawrenceville was where William Foster (father of Stephen) made his estate and where he supplied the land to establish this place of repose, limited to a simple square acre that would have been between contemporary Fisk and Main Streets, intended for soldiers assigned to the local arsenal but eventually opened to the entire community. The only evidence of that graveyard established in 1814 is a single, faded memorial stone in the basement of the Carnegie Library whose redbrick facade stolidly faces Butler Street.

Beneath the creaking wooden floorboards of that 165-year-old library, below the rows and rows of dusty volumes including Neville B. Craig's 1851 *The History of Pittsburgh, with a Brief Notice of Its Facilities of Communication, and Other Advantages for Commercial and Manufacturing Purposes* and Allen Becer's 1993 *Monster on the Allegheny and Other Lawrenceville Stories*, there is a badly chipped and damaged granite tombstone, its engravings amended by rain and wind to a fractured incompleteness. Becer identified that grave's former inhabitant, deducing from census records and the partial glyphs worn from entropy that a young boy named Henry Snowden, only fifteen months old at the time of his death, was entombed here in 1830. Snowden was moved with the rest of his family when development began, but the grave was left behind deep in the library basement. History was buried in the name of development, but in a place like Pittsburgh, the gravestones can't help but break through the newly poured concrete. As a metaphor it's almost shockingly obvious.

Lined with narrow and steep streets featuring restored Victorian townhomes that are all dark wood and stained glass, Lawrenceville has become a hipster destination, featuring over two dozen blocks of restaurants and bistros, galleries and boutiques, shops and bars, but before it was even a working-class Irish and then Polish neighborhood, it was a suburb of the growing metropolis, a slightly haunted place evoking the Victorian Gothic

A warning on the entrance to Lawrenceville's Allegheny Cemetery. *Wikimedia Commons, distributed under a CC-BY 2.0 license.*

as much as hipster Brooklyn. Not even gentrification can totally exorcize the dead, whether today or in the nineteenth century. History hangs about like early morning fog in the Allegheny Valley, though the presence of the dead beneath the streets of the neighborhood literalizes those hauntings a bit. "Everything that exists is possible only on the basis of a whole series of absences," writes British philosopher Mark Fisher in *Ghosts of My Life: Writings on Depression, Hauntology and Lost Futures*, "which precede and surround it." According to Fisher, modernity is haunted by both the past and by futures never consummated, so that the spectral metaphor remains a potent way of understanding the deep-seated malaise that permeates so much of contemporary experience. "A secret sadness lurks beneath the 21st century's forced smile," Fisher wrote, with more than a smidge of melancholy. As a philosopher, Fisher traded in abstractions, yet there is something perfectly macabre in the tangibility of one of the most dynamic neighborhoods in Pittsburgh atop this mass grave, itself the product of development more than a century ago.

Indeed, to wander down Butler Street is to see the hauntings of times past, not just in the Victorian townhomes but also in the ruins of the massive steel mills (long since repurposed) a few blocks closer to the Allegheny. This is something that I would compare to, but also differentiate from, what Fisher (drawing from previous philosophers) called "hauntology." I'd suggest that Pittsburgh offers a particular aesthetic and disposition that should be called the Allegheny Gothic. It's a sensibility that is aware of history's hauntings, where libraries are built on graveyards and homes on slag heaps, but beyond the prurient details, we're more poetically haunted by the presence of not just those past peoples but also that which motivated them, that which organized their days and lives, that which they believed in and that which they suffered for. At its height, Pittsburgh produced more steel than the entirety of the British Empire; such a history is not easily excised. Those who lived in Lawrenceville's fashionable homes were skilled laborers and puddlers in the mills, managers and accountants for Carnegie or Jones and Laughlin Steel. All of that is gone now; new development has replaced old, though the myths—or ghosts, rather—remain. There is an exceptional type of melancholy to this, the formerly most intrinsic and least dispensable of places now left to rust, even if, ironically, it's far more beautiful now, despite the bones of our ancestors beneath our feet.

What helps is that the age of our ascendancy was such a consummately Gothic time. The Gilded Age townhomes of Lawrenceville, with their vaguely steampunk aesthetic, are evidence of this, and the visual idiom

Pittsburgh is known for its surplus of so-called ghost signs, the faded advertisements left behind on buildings, sometimes nearly a century old, such as this sign Downtown. *Photograph by Chail19, distributed under a CC-BY 2.0 license.*

of such places—indeed, of the city itself—contributes a great deal to the Allegheny Gothic. As always, a lot of this has to do with the colors black and gold. On the logos of the Steelers, the Pirates and the Penguins is the same melancholic, morbid, macabre color scheme; Pittsburgh is the only city in the United States where all the professional sports teams share identical colors, which is the same hue as the city's official flag, drawn from the banner of the eighteenth-century British prime minister who gave the city its name, with Pitt's herald featuring a stone castle at its center, that symbol fluttering above government offices even today.

The second thing you must understand about the general mood of Pittsburgh is that it rains here, quite a lot. It's foggy, drizzly, often damp and frequently cold. For those of a San Diego predisposition, Pittsburgh must be purgatory, but as for myself, always drawn to the sepulcher and the cenotaph, the mausoleum and the memorial, the Allegheny Gothic is something that I take as my central attitude and aesthetic, sense and sensibility and my birthright. Maybe I'm only speaking for myself here, but my embrace of this mood neither comes from a deep wellspring of dissatisfaction nor manifests in some perennial sadness. Perhaps melancholy is simply the depression you enjoy, but for me, the Gothic environs of Pittsburgh evidence character, spirit, emotion. Where some may be partial to the cookie-cutter perfection of suburban tract homes in Charlotte or Phoenix, I find them positively creepy. Give me an old Victorian with shuttered windows, a skyscraper with gargoyles, an overcast drizzly day with rain falling on stone pathways, rather than oppressive, monotonous, uniform sunshine and the fake demeanors that engenders. Speaking subjectively, I think that the spirit of the Allegheny Gothic animates a certain personality type; for myself, there is sublimity in the introspections and meditations that the surrounding environment generates. Driving down damp Baum Boulevard late at night while WQED-FM plays the uncanny minimalism of Philip Glass's "Metamorphosis I" (incidentally, the composer lived on that street in 1962, working as a music teacher and cab driver) or listening on my phone to Meredith Monk's otherworldly *Book of Days* while I walk about the Highland Park reservoir on an autumn morning, I feel fully ensconced in the indescribable particulars of the Allegheny Gothic.

To get a sense of the Allegheny Gothic, devote an hour or so to wandering the grounds of Mellon Park at the intersection of Shadyside and Point Breeze, one of the United States' truly exemplary urban green spaces, preferably during a lonely winter morning. The grounds are set off from the long, straight ribbon of Fifth Avenue by a black wrought-iron fence, the middle punctuated by a grand opening into the park. Sloping upward from the street and back toward the comparatively quieter terminus of Beechwood Boulevard or the intersection with Shady Avenue, the bulk of this land was once the estate of banking magnate and scion of the famed (and at times nefarious) Mellon family. Here, Richard B. Mellon built a massive sixty-room Tudor mansion, the largest in Pittsburgh, with the land dedicated to the park being all that now remains. These gardens, which were the germinating seed for what would become Mellon Park, were designed by Olmsted Brothers, the same firm responsible for Central Park, and true to

Steps within Mellon Park. *Wikimedia Commons, distributed under a CC-BY 2.0 license.*

The upper wall of the Elizabethan flower garden in Mellon Park. *Photograph by Father Pitt, distributed under a CC1.0 license.*

its larger cousin in New York, the Pittsburgh park seamlessly combines the sylvan and the elegant, the bucolic and the urbane. Lots of those features, in keeping with the taste of a man born in the Victorian era, are still aspects of the park, including a terraced Elizabethan rose garden and a gorgeous flat promenade lined by a redbrick wall in the style of the English Renaissance that's covered in ivy.

At the far end of the promenade, set within the wall that separates the park from the grounds of the Pittsburgh Center for the Arts, is a Gothic white stone relief and a large fountain, decorated with unsettling statues of panpipe-playing cherubs and turtle grotesques. The relative height of the park's grounds affords a stunning view of much of the east end, underrated as skylines go when compared to that of Downtown but that, for me, is its equal in charms. There are the towers of East Liberty, both Victorian skyscrapers and new office towers alongside the blue dome of Motor Square Garden and the Gothic magnificence of the Presbyterian cathedral paid for by Mellon's brother Andrew as a sort of "fire escape" from the judgment he feared. In the distance, there is the campus of the Pittsburgh Theological Seminary, all steeples and redbrick buildings, as well as the twin spires of the abandoned Catholic Saints Peter and Paul Church, tiles now falling from their heights. The dome of the Beaux Arts former B'nai Israel Synagogue in East Liberty is visible not far beyond, and then the long line of Fifth, Penn, Baum, Centre, running east to west with the towers of Shadyside Hospital as well as the various high-rise apartments that constitute the east end skyline.

Obviously my own personal connection to these neighborhoods explains much of my affection, but standing in Mellon Park, whether by myself or in the midst of a crowded arts festival, with my family or listening to an outdoor concert, there is a sense of beauty that I inevitably connect to the Allegheny Gothic that permeates this heavy-stoned, dark brick, exhaust-stained Victorian city. I feel in the presence of all those specters of the past a certain power, a type of enchantment, that makes Pittsburgh feel more home to me than anywhere else that I've lived. For me, part of the charm of sites like the Elizabethan garden—currently in the midst of needed renovations—is precisely the studied decay it displays, the sense of entropy winning its war of attrition as seen in the crumbling bricks and the overgrown flower beds, a reminder of the seventeenth-century poet Robert Herrick's imploration to "gather ye rosebuds while ye may." Pittsburgh, I would claim, sometimes looks like something from an Edward Gorey illustration.

Nothing is a better representation of the Allegheny Gothic as aesthetic, sensibility and worldview than the absurd, bizarre, glorious and beautiful Cathedral of Learning. Arguably as much a symbol of the city as anything that I've discussed so far, the University of Pittsburgh's central building is categorically unique, an artifact of Pittsburgh idiosyncrasy. Conceived of by the visionary chancellor John Bowman in 1921, the limestone-encased, steel-latticed, forty-two-story skyscraper was completed in 1937; it's still the tallest building dedicated to education in the Western Hemisphere, as well as the second-tallest Gothic structure on Earth. Composed of medieval buttresses and grand entrances, gargoyles and grotesques, the golem of the cathedral dedicated to secular learning appears as if from Gotham, a testament to both the quixotism and hubris of Bowman, his dream to "make visible something of the spirit that was in the hearts of pioneers as, long ago, they sat in their log cabins and thought by candlelight of the great city that would sometime spread beyond their three rivers and that even then were starting to build."

Left: Fountain in Mellon Park.
Photograph by Father Pitt, distributed under a CC1.0 license.

Below: The Cathedral of Learning.
Photograph by Don Burkett, distributed under a CC-BY 2.0 license.

Bowman's phantasmagoria drew from the Gothic, the medieval, the Pre-Raphaelite: the fantasy of a cathedral in Cologne or Nantes constructed of steel girders and reinforced concrete. There is a bit of the cosplay in this kind of architecture, which is all the more glorious because of it. That Bowman's initiative was successful, the groundbreaking narrowly missing the 1929 stock market crash, with construction continuing despite the Great Depression, speaks to both his dedication and that of Pittsburgh's citizens, the majority of whom weren't college educated but who nonetheless raised money for the cathedral's construction as a matter of civic pride. That the style of the Cathedral of Learning was so fantastic—this building that features a three-story Common Room of high-flying buttresses, arched windows, massive iron candelabras, dark hidden passageways, secret nooks, strange and hermetic monastic carvings and mead hall–length tables rendered in Indiana limestone and Vermont slate—is part of what's strangely utopian about the Allegheny Gothic, a style that's not mournful but romantic, neither macabre but rather epic. From almost all the ninety neighborhoods, depending on height and perspective, there is normally a view that's possible of the Cathedral of Learning, solemn and solitary against the (still tall) towers of the rest of Oakland, standing like a sentry above the curving streets of the city, silhouetted in darkness at night save for

the light at its apex like a single unblinking eye. "Oh, I thought," writes Michael Chabon in his novel *The Mysteries of Pittsburgh* when a character espies the Cathedral of Learning, "the Emerald City in the twelfth century."

Naturally the Cathedral of Learning is haunted. How could it be otherwise? Urban legend most vociferously focuses on a particular locale within the building that apparently houses said specters—not unpredictably, one of the famed Nationality Rooms that line the perimeter of the first and third floors of the Common Room. As part of his fundraising strategy, Bowman inaugurated the Nationality Room program, whereby each of the individual ethnicities then filling Pittsburgh's working-class neighborhoods would sponsor a classroom dedicated to their homeland, afterward being responsible for the design and upkeep of said

A postcard from 1945 showing the Cathedral of Learning at night. *Courtesy of the Boston Public Library Tichnor Brother Collection.*

spaces. Eventually there would be thirty-one such rooms—they're still being dedicated today—but the earliest include an English Room, Irish Room, Italian Room, Polish Room, German Room and so on. The Early American Room, honoring not a foreign nation but the colonial history of this one, is the odd room out and the supposed locus of paranormal activity within the cathedral. Constructed from white pine disassembled from a Hull, Massachusetts residence of the seventeenth century, the Early American Room is as if a New England cabin manifested from the ether in the midst of Pittsburgh.

Two stories tall—the only such room among the thirty-six of which that can be said—the Early American Room features various implements of everyday colonial New England life, including a log-burning fireplace, a spinning wheel and a waffle iron. The room's upper story is hidden, its entrance revealed by a concealed latch, with the second floor decorated in the manner of a nineteenth-century bedroom. According to tour groups, docents and custodians, this place is the dark kernel within the massive edifice of the cathedral, the dwelling place of poltergeists and other damned phenomena. The smell of freshly baking bread from the fireplace, the ruffling of the quilt on the four-poster bed, the rocking of an empty cradle, shadows cast from nothingness—all have been reported experiences. Describing the nation that this room commemorates, critic Leslie Fiedler notes in *Love and Death in the American Novel* that the United States is "bewilderingly and embarrassingly, a Gothic fiction, nonrealistic and negative, sadist and melodramatic—a literature of darkness and the grotesque in a land of light and affirmation." Whether or not a ghost haunts the Early American Room, Fiedler suggests that America haunts all of us, that the deep history of this land forged through violence and exploitation indelibly marks our very souls, whether literally or figuratively. How could it be any different in the city that was responsible for this nation's earliest and greatest prosperity?

Perhaps the unhappy poltergeists of the Cathedral of Learning are imported specters, brought in with the oak planks and bubbled glass of the New England house that now finds itself several hundred miles south and west with an entire skyscraper constructed around it, but there are plenty of homegrown Pittsburgh ghosts as well. The ruins of the Pittsburgh City Tuberculosis Hospital, the Troy Hill Firehouse, the William Penn Hotel and Point Park University's original Playhouse Theater have all had their share of paranormal visitation. On the twenty-third floor of the gilded, elegant corridors of the William Penn Hotel, which leers out over the bustle of Downtown streets, guests have recorded inexplicable cool spots and maniacal

The Early American Room in the Cathedral of Learning. *Photograph by Daderot, distributed under a CC-BY 2.0 license.*

laughter in the pitch-blackness of night; performers and technicians at the Playhouse have encountered a far more inexplicable rageful ball of glowing light that bounces off walls and down corridors, appropriately nicknamed the Red Meanie.

Most terrifying, however, are the hauntings within Clayton, the twenty-three-room Italianate Victorian mansion of the coke magnate robber baron Henry Clay Frick. Among the grand estates that were built by Pittsburgh industrialists who made Point Breeze the greatest concentration of wealth in American history, Clayton is the only one which remains. H.J. Heinz's grand Penn Avenue mansion Greenlawn only survives in the form of a wrought-iron gate that runs for several blocks past the modest middle-class homes that replaced his estate; George Westinghouse's palace, the first residence in history to be outfitted for electric lights, featuring an actual oil drill on the property, has since been turned into a city park; the only evidence of Andrew Carnegie's castle is the street named for him (and his carriage house). Clayton alone stands, and true to its owner's disposition, something wicked still wanders its heavily carpeted, wood-paneled hallways. Depressions appearing on an empty bed, the sound of muffled footsteps in the night, the forced, angry breathing of somebody—*something*—in an otherwise quiet room. Frick, alone among the industrialists of Pittsburgh, had no pretensions to virtue, philanthropic or otherwise. He wore his gold gospel of economic exploitation as if a solemn badge and had no use for superstitions like charity or grace: a hard man in a hard city, rightly hated by the citizens who lived here and toiled in his coke works or in the steel mills of Carnegie, which he administered for a time.

It's another rather literal metaphor, the robber baron haunting his old manor, for Pittsburgh can be a necropolis of grand ideas, of those metanarratives of industrial capitalism that haunt us like a curse. More than anything, we're haunted by the idea of the Iron City, of what it represents and what it was. If you're on a tour of Clayton today, for it is a wonderful museum, you can view that bed that supposedly shows warm indentation from a body invisible and consider that it was here that Frick had to convalesce after he was shot twice at point-blank range and stabbed multiple times in a botched assassination attempt in his Downtown office. That Frick endured such unlikely odds for survival conjures more than a mere odor of sulfur, so perhaps his punishment is to forever wander this house with its

Henry Clay Frick's estate, Clayton. *Photograph by Daderot, distributed under a CC-BY 2.0 license.*

thick oriental rugs and heavy English oak, oils by Peter Paul Reubens and pastels by Claude Monet, the red velvet drapes still stained with Pittsburgh soot, all of it guiding the specter through these halls that he once knew so well. To encounter other ghosts, just cross into the park named for Frick, wander the several miles down to the banks of the Monongahela and look across the river to the town of Homestead. There, on the site of a Carnegie Steel plant that made men like Frick very rich, are ten solitary smokestacks rising up like redbrick fingers from the earth. Each one commemorates the ten men murdered by Pinkertons during the strike of 1892, their deaths directly attributable to the orders of Frick. "I do not think I will die," said Frick after he was shot by an anarchist's bullet in retaliation for his criminal acts, "but whether I do or not, the company will pursue the same policies." Now that site of labor's martyrdom is crowded with shopping malls and chain restaurants. We're haunted still, though I'm not sure by what.

Chapter 9

FRIES ON EVERYTHING

With limestone cliffs overlooking the Celtic Sea and sandy beaches on the Bristol Channel, Devonshire features heaths growing heather and gorse and fishing villages with names like Ilfracombe and Lynmouth—it is absurdly British. Because of that, a turn-of-the-twentieth-century Anglophilic Pittsburgh city planner some 3,595 miles to the west appropriated the county's name when laying out streets. Appropriately lined by Tudor mansions with cross-hatch facades and the inlaid stained glass that marked upper-class homes of Pittsburgh, Devonshire Street was one of the city's toniest addresses. As neighborhoods filled with immigrants from Dublin and Naples, Krakow and Budapest (as well as Charleston and Biloxi), Devonshire Street advertised Anglo-Saxon connotations. Ironically it was the son of Sicilian immigrants, a chef named Frank Blandi, who immortalized the street.

In 1935, while working in the kitchen of the similarly Anglophilic Stratford Club, Blandi invented Pittsburgh's singular white tablecloth dish—the rich, calorie-laden pantomime of WASP cooking that is the glorious, ungodly and almost extinct Turkey Devonshire. Apocryphally, Blandi was looking for an English-sounding name to match his English-sounding restaurant, eventually saw the sign and took the name as if the dish had always come from the land of Cornish pasties and white pudding. Regional dishes often have a mythologized creation story, a moment in which serendipitous ingenuity lends itself to deliciousness. Some local cuisine seems eternal—who invented New England clam chowder, the New York big slice or the California fish

A Turkey
Devonshire.
*Picture courtesy
of Richard Kelly
Photography and*
Belt Magazine.

taco? But other dishes emerge from the firmament itself. Think of Anchor
Bar proprietor Teressa Bellissimo, who one upstate New York evening in
1964 whipped up a late-night snack for her son's college friends, coating
fried chicken wings with a mixture of butter and Frank's RedHot sauce, a
side of blue cheese dressing as a dip, and celery as a garnish, thus inventing
the buffalo wing. Or when sometime in the early thirties, South Philly
brothers Pat and Harry Olivieri first frizzled sheet beef, onions and peppers,
melted some provolone on top (later Cheez Whiz) and threw it all on top of
a hoagie roll so as to create the first cheesesteak. The Devonshire doesn't
have the reach of the buffalo wing or the aura of the cheesesteak; you can't
find it at Applebee's, nor is it a Superbowl staple, but it's among Pittsburgh's
gastronomic creations, though often forgotten.

"When we first started working on the Devonshire, it didn't look like it
does now," recalled Blandi in 1983 to *Pittsburgh Press* food writer Marilyn
McDevitt Rubin. "It was flat." But as God pulled the round earth out of the
inky undifferentiated blackness of space, so too would Blandi tinker until the
Devonshire emerged. The exact nature of this alchemy is unknown—what
inspired Blandi and why this particular recipe depends on who is doing the
telling. His grandniece Kim Ifft, who used to work at Alexander's Bistro in
Bloomfield, is quoted in *Pittsburgh Magazine* as hypothesizing that for tired
kitchen staff who'd been "setting up, cooking, cleaning for people, you're
hungry. It's late at night. You'd say, 'Cook, make us something.'…Well,
maybe there's some leftover turkey. Maybe there's some gravy. And you want
to fancy it up. I can see how this gets better and better as you keep playing

with it." Regardless of the how, Blandi's final result was sublime: a cassoulet dish lined with toasted white bread, on which is layered a hefty portion of roasted turkey, all of which is drenched in viscous cheddar cheese sauce, crowned with a cruciform of thick-cut bacon and then, as if mocking God Himself, two or three thin tomato slices. A thin sprinkling of paprika and Parmesan anoints the top. The whole thing is baked at medium temperature for several minutes until the cheese turns the enchanted glowing hue of an industrial orange sunset. Ideally, the surface should crust slightly, reminiscent of the browned portions of macaroni and cheese or the French onion soup where the Gruyère bubbles over onto the crock's lip. Some recipes allow for crabmeat, shrimp or even asparagus, but it should be noted that vodka and vermouth isn't a martini. Technically, the dish is an open-faced sandwich, but that's like calling the Empire State Building an office complex or the Golden Gate Bridge a water crossing. Done right, it should be well over two thousand calories. Culinary agnostics may note that Blandi's recipe bears more than a passing resemblance to Louisville's fabled Hot Brown sandwich or the cheesy British classic known as Welsh rarebit. That's of no account—creation myths have to create out of *something*. Besides, despite the Devonshire's slightly fussy and pretentious name, it's a truth universally acknowledged that it sounds infinitely more appetizing than whatever it is that "Hot Brown" describes.

Blandi would have a half-century-long career as, effectively, Pittsburgh's earliest celebrity chef, working at the Park Schenley Hotel, the Pittsburgh Playhouse and, finally, Le Mont, which served *Mad Men*–era haute cooking and remains a bastion of Franco-Normcore cuisine. Unknown outside of the region, the Devonshire was omnipresent on the menus of finer restaurants. The classic seafood restaurant Poli's, not far from the Squirrel Hill tunnel, widely known for both its bronze-plated lobster doorknobs and its tank of actual ill-fated crustaceans, served it until closing in 2005. Nino's on Craig

Frank Blandi in chef's hat in front of the Park Schenley hotel. *Courtesy of LeMont Restaurant.*

Street in Oakland had it on the menu, as did its successor More's, an old-school restaurant where the elderly waiters had tuxedos, the walls were covered in Italianate paintings of varying quality and the Caesar dressing was made tableside. It closed in 2010. The more intimate red sauce joint Alexander's in Bloomfield's Little Italy was one of the last to serve the dish—that is, until 2020, when they turned off their stoves. It endures on a handful of menus in Western Pennsylvania, offered at a few diners, delis and dives as an exercise in nostalgia. Local food writer Dave Forman, who operates the blog *David the Gastronome*, told me that today, it's often treated as a "fancier club sandwich, probably made with the same terrible, overcooked and dry turkey, using bacon that's left over from morning breakfast and topped with a cheese sauce that has little cheese in it." For me, that's neither here nor there, because I will defend the Turkey Devonshire as a contribution of Pittsburgh's singular *socio-gastronomy*.

Boston is clambakes and chowder, New York pastrami on rye and water dogs, Chicago T-bones and baked potatoes, Los Angeles tofu bowls and bulgogi burritos. What the stereotypes hold about a region's favored foods tells us much about how an area wishes to be seen—or at least about how it is seen. Identity is often as much about what goes into the mouth as the words that come out of it. The French philosopher Roland Barthes in his 1979 essay "Towards a Psychosociology of Contemporary Food Consumption" asks rather prosaically, "What is food?" and answers that it is "a system of communication, a body of images, a protocol of usages, situations, and behaviors." Few people eat only to satiate appetite; what we choose to ingest comes from the traditions of our families and communities, how we choose to present ourselves to the wider world and religious and ethical considerations (not to mention based on if we think something will taste good). In asking what Pittsburgh food is, our questions are not just culinary but also anthropological, sociological, philosophical. There are certain connotations that the Steel City evokes, and those same connotations are connected to the dishes associated with the region. The city of stick-to-the-ribs Eastern European food, all meat and potatoes washed down with a shot of Canadian Club Rye and a cold can of Iron City. Considering Barthes, such food communicates an understanding of Pittsburgh as a working-class hamlet, a no-frills, no-fuss, unpretentious metropolis where there's not enough time between shifts to do anything other than shove your French fries into your sandwich and char the steak on the outside while leaving its interior bloody raw. A masculine gastronomy, if you will. This is, as should be expected, a gross simplification that nonetheless has within it a shred of familiarity. So,

Neon sign from Klein's, another much-missed Pittsburgh normcore cuisine staple, as photographed in 1989. *Courtesy the Library of Congress.*

Primanti Brothers, arguably the most famous of Pittsburgh restaurants. *Photograph by Dllu, distributed under a CC-BY 2.0 license.*

for example, among the most well-regarded of new restaurants in Pittsburgh is an establishment named Apteka on Penn Avenue between Bloomfield and Garfield, a sign of the city's more cosmopolitan dining scene, as it was named a finalist for the James Beard Awards. Unsurprisingly for Pittsburgh, it's a Polish restaurant—a vegan one.

Twenty restaurants within Pittsburgh now feature a Michelin star, with *Zagat* ranking Pittsburgh the nation's best food city in 2016. Its reputation has been burnished over the past two decades, as establishments in the Big Burrito Restaurant Group from hip Casbah in Shadyside and swanky Eleven in the Strip have brought a more sophisticated cookery to Pittsburghers' palates, while upstarts like the Richard DeShantz Group have opened restaurants such as the cheeky sushi bar gi-jin and funky Tako Torta, both Downtown. Meanwhile, the long stretch of blocks radiating out from the intersection of Forbes and Murray in Squirrel Hill has transformed the center of Pittsburgh's Jewish community into America's newest Chinatown, with dozens of restaurants devoted to every variety of Asian cuisine, from Korean fried chicken to hot pot, dim sum to bubble tea. At Pusadee's Garden

Apteka, Pittsburgh's James Beard Award–nominated Polish vegan restaurant. *Photograph by Tony Webster, distributed under a CC-BY 2.0 license.*

on Butler in Lawrenceville, a beautifully minimalist space serving reinvented Thai cuisine, there is more of an evocation of California cool than beers at a VFW; within Fet Fisk's Nordic chill space serving postmodern Scandinavian food, there is little sartorial resemblance to microwaved halupki at the Knights of Columbus or baked ziti in a Liberty Avenue red sauce place.

Yet per Barthes's observation about the mythic nature of food, it's hard not to notice that old tastes hardly disappear, as several of the city's well-regarded newer restaurants—the Speckled Egg, Bridges and Bourbon, Meat & Potatoes—are "New American Restaurants" where the menu might feature bone marrow or sweetmeats and the boilermaker is made with top-shelf liquor but the vibe is still very much potbellied and bearded Pittsburgh. "If there are scholars who hope to study how a vibrant food culture can help radically transform an American city," writes Jeff Gordinier in a 2015 *New York Times* piece, "the time to do that is right now, in real time, in the place that gave us Heinz ketchup." All of that is well and good—I'd be disingenuous if I didn't say that part of me was proud of the national attention, and most practically, I do appreciate all the great new restaurants. Yet arguably, there has always been an underappreciated genius to Pittsburgh's food scene, where as much as we can enjoy the arrival of dining establishments like Umi and Morcilla, we can also mourn the demise of More's and Poli's.

Besides, the fries-on-everything stereotype owes as much to the Food Network's endless featuring of a certain restaurant chain that began in the Strip District as it does to reality. There has always been elegant food in Pittsburgh, even if now it's a bit more democratically available. As a representative example, consider the rich decadence of Crabmeat Hoelzel. As simple as a sonnet and perfect as a martini, Crabmeat Hoelzel was invented by master chef Nicholas Colletti within the private and rarefied world of the Duquesne Club—all mahogany, Oriental rugs and nineteenth-century oil paintings—where captains of industry dined, such as the president of the Pittsburgh Screw and Bolt Company who leant his name to this dish. Still served at the Duquesne Club today, Crabmeat Hoelzel is ridiculously easy to prepare: a liberal portion of jumbo lump meat from Maryland, tossed in a dressing of extra virgin olive oil, a dash of cider and tarragon vinegar and a prodigious grinding of black pepper, all of it allowed to chill for twenty-four hours in the refrigerator. Maybe some chives if you're the baroque sort, served on melba toast if you wish to slightly tamper with perfection.

Crabmeat Hoelzel, gloriously old-fashioned, is a triumph of mid-century cuisine, a dish that trusts completely in the purity of its ingredients and respects the simplicity of them combined appropriately. Ironically, that exact same principle is on display in another gastronomic delight, the titular Pittsburgh Salad, which is found on the menu of far more local bars than the Duquesne Club's effete Crabmeat Hoelzel happens to be. There are variations, of course, but in general, the algorithm narrating the construction of a Pittsburgh Salad is straightforward: a heap of painfully suburban chopped iceberg lettuce (never arugula, never Boston Bibb), maybe some diced cherry tomatoes or cucumbers, possibly a few croutons, all garnished with a heavy pile of shredded sharp cheddar, sliced steak (flank, rare) and two handfuls of steaming hot, right-out-of-the-fryer fries, all doused in an obscenity of dressing, with my preference being blue cheese. For some reason, there is a strange distaste that some visitors have for the French fries on sandwiches and salads phenomenon, a turning up the nose at what's objectively a nonexotic phenomenon (have they never gotten a gyro before?). I'm studiedly ambivalent about fries on a hoagie, but on the Pittsburgh Salad, the delightful disjunct of temperatures and textures—tender steak and crisp lettuce, cold cucumbers and hot fries—is objectively a triumph.

Above: Exterior of the Duquesne Club, site of the Crabmeat Hoelzel's invention. *Photograph by Lee Paxton, distributed under a CC-BY 2.0 license.*

Left: This is a salad. *Photograph by Neeta Lind, distributed under a CC-BY 2.0 license.*

Then there are the classic Yinzer dishes increasingly endangered, such as the chipped chopped ham barbecue sandwich, which every native Pittsburgher has certainly eaten—but most likely not in the past year. Composed of the aforementioned lunch meat most associated with the now-closed chain Isaly's (hence its relative rarity), the chipped chopped ham barbecue sandwich may not compete with its cousins in North Carolina or Kansas City, but as a chain reaction of salt and sweet, it's still filling while also delivering the requisite caloric dopamine high. Chipped chopped ham is its own unique offal loaf, a kind of greasy, semitransparent, thin-cut variation on SPAM, flecked with gelatinous fat the color of a pig's innards. Pat Kiger of *Pittsburgh Magazine* gives a tutorial on the manufacture of this mystery meat made of "fat and muscle trimmings...[which is] placed in a special machine, and tumbled to separate the protein (which, when the mean is reshaped, will act as a binding agent)," describing the resultant product, which is an astounding 17 percent fat, as resembling a "sort of flesh-colored pudding." Yum! Made of ground chunks and trimmings, chipped chopped ham is honest in its very name, a food that, while it elects not to tell you what exactly it's composed of, will at least be blunt that it's not going to be anything particularly appetizing. Nonetheless, when folded into little origami piles on a potato roll and slathered in barbecue sauce or ketchup, with maybe a few Heinz pickle slices on top, this sodium bomb of a sandwich is undeniably a comforting dish, the equivalent of a warm and greasy hug from a childhood friend you only see every few years but still hold a fondness for.

Even more intrinsically Pittsburgh than chipped chopped ham is a desert that has seen a resurgence in the last few years as a staple of hipster irony, even though when served at summer picnics it was intended to be completely genuine. Strawberry Pretzel Salad is a vestige of the postwar desire to find as many usages for gelatin as possible, but while Magic Jell-O Desert and Ambrosia either disappeared or only endure in regional variations, the Pittsburgh dessert hobbles onward in sundry corners of local restaurants and homes, a coelacanth of 1950s dining. A kind of trifle that has a crushed pretzel base, piled with a sour cream and whipped cream center and topped with gelatin-imprisoned strawberries, this gently surreal treat poises salty and sweet in an agreeable arrangement almost Taoist in its paradoxes.

There are, thankfully, still some dining rituals that are in no danger of disappearing anytime soon. In that vein, a few words must be spent to examine the phenomenon of the Pittsburgh fish sandwich. Because it takes a good seven hours to drive from Pittsburgh to the Atlantic—even Lake Erie is three hours north—there is a certain irony to the popularity of this sandwich, but perhaps by a particular Lenten logic it makes sense that we desire that which is most hard to acquire. Firmly landlocked, Pittsburgh lacks the aquatic resources that allow for the New England lobster roll or the Chesapeake crab cake. That, however, hasn't stopped the deep-fried cod sandwich from being the underrated hero of Pittsburgh culinary identity. A staple in not just seafood restaurants but also dive bars, diners

Fried cod with the requisite Heinz ketchup. *Photo courtesy of Community Kitchen Pgh and* Belt Magazine.

and delis, the thickly breaded and preferably massive deep-fried prefrozen cod or haddock sandwich is ideally as filling as it is overwhelming on first inspection. Institutions like the Squirrel Hill pizzeria Mineo's offer the "Codfather" during Lent, while the now sadly closed hip Shadyside bar the Harris Grill (famed for Tuesday "Bacon Night") once offered the "Monongahela Mullet" (because the fish hangs over the bun).

How much the popularity of the fish sandwich and its eponymous fry owes to Pittsburgh's status as a particularly Catholic city is worth conjecture. Unsurprisingly when considering the wave of southern and eastern European immigration that redefined Pittsburgh's demographics in the first half of the twentieth century, the metropolitan era is tied alongside New York City and Boston as the "most Catholic" major city in the United States in terms of per capita percentage, according to a 2014 poll conducted by the Public Religion Research Institute, with 36 percent of respondents identifying as such. In such an environment, Lenten traditions extend beyond the diocese and into Protestant churches and VFW Halls, school gymnasiums and corner bars. As in many cities, overall church attendance and denominational membership has declined, yet the fish sandwich remains. More than that, the fish fry is a vestige of a Pittsburgh that's largely in eclipse, a reminder of the city's mid-century economic height, when union membership and ethnic community ties led to a high standard of living. Uncommodified and proudly local, the fish fry exists beyond the dictates of neoliberal homogenization. To enjoy fried cod and coleslaw in the basement of a church is to refuse a type of gentrification, it's to resist the economic forces attempting to transform Pittsburgh into something palatable to out-of-town real estate developers. Returning to

my favorite sandwich, though the
Devonshire sounds gastronomically
excessive to a generation raised
on kale and quinoa (or the idea of
kale and quinoa), Blandi's dish was
no exercise in Guy Fieri decadence.
Forman quips that it's the "high-
class answer to liver and onions.
It made folks feel special because
they were eating something out of
a clay pot that had been baked."
In mid-century Pittsburgh, the
Devonshire was taken as an elegant

Pittsburgh in a meal. *Photograph by Dominik Schwind, distributed under a CC-BY 2.0 license.*

recipe, enjoyed by the same women and men who ordered heavy dishes
like chicken Kiev and steak Daniel, with vichyssoise or tomato juice as
an appetizer. So far, there is no McCaffery Real Estate–sponsored fish fry
offering tuna nigiri at the Strip Terminal. Sadly, there doesn't seem to
be a Devonshire on the menu of any of those new restaurants down on
Smallman Street either.

When Pittsburgh's culinary scene is discussed in the national media, it's
still often as a shot-and-beer town partial to pierogies, kielbasa and pastrami
sandwiches piled high with fries and coleslaw—more Good Friday fish fry
than brunch at the 21 Club. Or, conversely, Pittsburgh is celebrated as the
gentrified Rust Belt comeback story, a foodie mecca for the New American
cuisine, with *Zagat* namechecking hip new establishments like Shadyside's
Chaz and Odette and East Liberty's Whitfield. But between the Scylla and
Charybdis of Primanti Brothers and molecular gastronomy lay the Turkey
Devonshire, too fussy to be mere bar food but too stodgy to be on the menu
of any restaurant catering to a hip clientele. Many adjectives can be used
to describe the Devonshire—antiquated, excessive, cardiac insalubrious.
Forman described it as a "salt bomb" without balance or nuance. But it
is reassuring. Tasting like a cross between mac and cheese and a turkey
sandwich, the Devonshire is the definition of comfort food. I'll also add
that there's something that's *playful* about the Devonshire. What I'd suggest
is that the almost over-the-top WASPiness of the meal is indicative of
Blandi's Italian American culinary humor. The white bread, the cheese,
the bacon, the turkey, *the goddamn name*. Only mayonnaise could have made
the Devonshire Whiter. Yet just as John Coltrane deconstructed the vanilla
melody of "My Favorite Things" and made it a baroque jazz masterpiece

or Mel Brooks appropriated the Western into the Borscht Belt brilliance of *Blazing Saddles*, so too did Blandi zhuzh away the bland of the turkey sandwich with some béchamel and smoked paprika broiled at 350 degrees. More than comfort, what the Devonshire represents is how somebody can come to the United States, see what's being offered and make it better.

Chapter 10

KEEP PITTSBURGH WEIRD

E very June, as if with an inner magnetic sense, they arrive from Atlanta and New York, Minneapolis and Seattle, thousands of them descending on the David L. Lawrence Convention Center: large, anthropomorphic, humanoid red foxes with white-striped tails, wooly brown bears, green-eyed black cats and panting golden retrievers. Spring in Pittsburgh is mating season, for this is when the furries return. Steel City Anthrocon—the largest national convention dedicated to the furry fandom, a subculture in which people ascribe animal characteristics to their own personality and dress in uniquely personal, bespoke costumes (to which a certain sexual adventurism has often been ascribed)—has been annually held in Pittsburgh since 2006. Anthrocon draws artists, craftsmen and performers but also accountants, nurses and teachers who are attracted to the furry lifestyle. Officially the largest recognized convention of its type, Anthrocon injects around $7 million into the local economy every summer, all while raising money for appropriately animal-themed nonprofits like the South Hills Pet Rescue, the Western Pennsylvania Humane Society and the Pittsburgh Zoo and PPG Aquarium. Mike Larson of WPXI writes that local politicians and business owners are invested in the furries always "coming back to Pittsburgh," with a special interest in them bringing "their purses and wallets" as well. Viewing the city's embrace of our furry fans as only transactionally economic would be a mistake, however, for on the whole I've encountered a pretty universal truism: Pittsburghers love the furries.

The furries arrive in Pittsburgh at Anthrocon 2014. *Wikimedia Commons, distributed under a CC-BY 2.0 license.*

At their first meeting following the COVID-19 pandemic, Anthrocon was even addressed by county executive Rich Fitzgerald, who told the assembled, "Every summer we really enjoy having you come and visit and learn about some of the great things that this city and this region have to offer," adding with what seemed to be genuine emotion directed at this assemblage of human-sized dogs, cats, birds and reptiles, "We missed you for a couple years." For those of us who are not furries, it's hard not to think that dressing as an animal is, well, sort of strange, but the glory is that we don't need to understand to accept; we don't need to belong to welcome. In an article for WESA, journalist Katie Blackley quotes Kathy Gerbasi, a social psychologist at Niagara County Community College who researches the community as well as participating in it, who said that for many furries, the "fandom is the first place where they found belongingness....Here's a place where you can sort of be yourself."

As many conference-goers venture out, they often speak of a friendliness from locals (the vast majority of whom are not furries). A furry from Massachusetts who goes by the name Splittbatt told Blackley that they had "fallen in love with the city," and that love is unironically returned, for indeed, the arrival of the furries feels like carnival, the genuine enthusiasm of the participants inserting a wonderfully surreal tenor into the humid Pittsburgh June days. If there is a lesson in the mutual affection between Pittsburgh and her furries, it's that the city—sometimes maligned as provincial, insular or parochial—is also far stranger than is assumed, that there is a deep-seated embrace of the weird here that I'd argue is unparalleled in the United States. At a time when social conservatism is encroaching throughout the country with the banning of books and drag shows, there is a lesson about tolerance that the Steel City can offer. Bumper stickers implore residents to "Keep Austin Weird" or "Keep Boulder Weird," but the furries didn't pick Austin or Boulder; they picked us. You don't see "Keep Pittsburgh Weird" bumper stickers here—it would never even occur to us, because we simply are.

There are any number of weird places in Pittsburgh, little vortices and nexuses between the profane world and something unseen. Consider making a pilgrimage to such less-visited historical sites as the stretch of the Monongahela River near the Homestead Waterfront and underneath the Glenwood Bridge where, early in 1956, an Air Force B-25 slowly glided over the brown water and crashed beneath the surface in full view of hundreds of workers changing shift at the steel mill. Only four of the six onboard made it to shore, but virtually all of the plane itself somehow disappeared, even while there are many who swear that the following night, barges arrived to retrieve all the broken machinery (and whatever it was carrying). Meanwhile, the U.S. government maintained that the vehicle had somehow fully disappeared in only twenty feet of water. Maybe it had something to do with an incident only nine years later in the Westmoreland County town of Kecksburg, where a fireball that was seen across several midwestern states crashed. The *Greensburg Tribune-Review* reported that the "area where the object landed was immediately sealed off on the order of the U.S. Army and State Police officials, in anticipation of a 'close inspection' of whatever may have fallen." Hypotheses about what it was range from a meteor to the debris of a felled Soviet satellite, but obviously the more interesting explanation is of the extraterrestrial variety, the possibility of desiccated gray alien corpses littering farmland too evocative to dismiss.

Should downed UFOs not be your preferred flavor of oddity, Pittsburgh has any number of cultural institutions beyond the expected candidates to investigate. The Museum of Post-Natural History in Garfield has exhibits of genetically tinkered creatures ranging from a mouse with a human ear growing out of its back to the taxidermized body of a goat adapted to produce spider silk. If your focus tends more toward the arts, than you could spend some time at Randyland in the Mexican War Streets, an institution

Keeping it weird in Mars, Pennsylvania. *Photograph by Michael Salone, distributed under a CC-BY 2.0 license.*

The colorful front of Randyland in the Mexican War Streets. *Wikimedia Commons, distributed under a CC-BY 2.0 license.*

named for its creator, outsider artist Randy Gilson, who transformed his entire townhome into an ultraviolet edifice of pure vibrant color, a building that in gray Pittsburgh shines in pastel blue and neon red, the entire thing covered in found objects and curated materials. Not far from Randyland, there's a similar transformation in the form of the Troy Hill Art Houses, three abandoned residences completely altered into what feel like avant-garde haunted houses for adults, open twenty-four hours a day. "San Francisco is manufactured weirdness," said a respondent to Jim Crotty in his lexicon *How to Talk America: A Guide to Our Native Tongues*, concluding that "Pittsburgh just has natural weirdness."

Weirdness resides not in places for the most part but rather in people. A big part of the gentle surrealism of Pittsburgh is due to the personality of its residents. Pittsburgh has often been libeled as "Midwest nice," but the reality is far more complicated. As a result of its liminal geographic identity, Pittsburghers both draw from as well as reject many of the personality traits associated with the three major regions that roughly converge here. Friendlier than many northeasterners, brusquer than most midwesterners and more tolerant than southerners, Pittsburghers most fully value a way of interacting with others that's entirely our own. "Pittsburgh friendly," it must be emphasized, is dissimilar to both the passive-aggressive friendliness of the stereotypical genteel South and the slightly pathological friendliness of the "Aw, shucks" Midwest. Rather than passive aggressive, Pittsburgh friendliness is often simply aggressive-aggressive (our conversations can sound like fights). There is an amazing range in interactions with Pittsburghers, the full gauntlet of human emotion. Asking somebody for directions will result in intricate instructions based on landmarks decades gone, perhaps interspersed with their mother's recipe for rigatoni and an intricate parsing of who you might both know in common. Follow-up questions could then generate rage, which will ultimately turn back into friendliness. Unlike stoic and taciturn New Englanders, Pittsburghers will talk—quite a bit. Sitting on a barstool in Pittsburgh, you will learn about not just somebody's favorite quarterbacks but also tragedies that befell them, secret desires and shames and their changing opinions on existential dilemmas. I once got into a conversation with the Verizon guy about generational positions on parenting, and I talked with the checkout woman in Home Depot about how amazing the abstract concept of language is. The metropolitan area whose residents most remind me of Pittsburghers isn't a midwestern locale but rather New York. There is a kindredness of eccentricity that's present in both.

That raw, naked possibility of sharing metaphysical conjectures with somebody on the bus is the gasoline of Pittsburgh weirdness; it's also a testament to a certain understanding of humanity whereby friendliness is not mere social strategy but an empathetic curiosity about these fellow people who occupy this time and space with us. In our current epoch of unprecedented social division, stratification and atomization, there is a certain Pittsburgh weirdness that can act as antidote, where the question "How you doing?" expects a response and two people can bleed emotion with one another in the time it takes to finish an Iron City. "I am the mate and companion of people," wrote the poet Walt Whitman in *Leaves of Grass*, "all just as immortal and fathomless as myself." A Brooklynite who spent years in Jersey and Philadelphia, Whitman's declaration strikes me as very Pittsburgh, a type of friendliness that's copacetic with the innate weirdness of being alive. Weirdness is in short supply throughout the United States, or when it does emerge, it's instantly commodified and drained of any of its subversive potential. America used to have many "Republics of Dreams," places like Greenwich Village and the Castro, Haight Ashbury and the East Village, but now they're largely tourist attractions, places to stop at a Chase Manhattan Bank on your way to eat at Sweetgreen.

I'm not claiming that Pittsburgh is immune to such gentrification—a visit to the Southside Works will disabuse me of that—but speaking only of my own small corner in Squirrel Hill, the great American tradition of being an eccentric, an oddball, a weirdo still exists. Possessing far more cerebral tweediness than we're sometimes given credit for (we compete with Boston in number of PhDs), the center of the world that is the confluence of Forbes and Murray at the heart of Squirrel Hill has always had a certain crunchy edge to it. Characters that I remember from growing up include the

The much-missed Beehive Coffee Shop on East Carson Street, closed in 2018, but once the capital of the South Side when that neighborhood was entirely weirder than it is today. *Photograph by Piotrus, distributed under a CC-BY 2.0 license.*

elderly Hawaiian-shirted man with an epic beard worthy of Whitman who would sit in the back of the 61C Café parsing out kabbalistic formula on napkins, the classically trained violinist who would play Roma songs under the black-and-white marquee of the Manor Theater, the beret-wearing gallery owner who used to sell compositions on Forbes, the U.S. history teacher who drove a Volvo with contradictory political bumper stickers and whoever still does the complex mathematical calculations in chalk on the library's outer walls late at night. All this is predicated on a glorious type of freedom that cities exult in: a genuine belief that people should be let to do what they want to do as long as it's not hurting anyone and that maybe there is some value in what they're doing anyhow. For me, Squirrel Hill was always a neighborhood of intellectuals and artists, academics and mystics, made up of used bookstores and kosher restaurants, coffee shops and curio stores, and even as demographics change and the pizza shop becomes a bubble tea place or the delicatessen a Sichuan hot pot joint, the fundamental character remains the same. All of this, and still without a Sweetgreen or Chipotle in sight.

Lest this all just be read as naive romanticizing by a native son who should travel more, I'll call on the authority of two of the greatest idiosyncratic iconoclasts in American arts and letters. Both of them—the great avatar of cinematic avant-garde tactlessness, director John Waters, and the baroque experimental rock genius and leader of the Talking Heads, David Byrne—are Baltimoreans, and I don't think that their love of Pittsburgh is a mistake. Charm City on the Chesapeake Bay is perhaps one of the few cities that can rival Pittsburgh in weirdness. Waters with his pencil-thin Vincent Price mustache, a man partial to zebra print jackets, and Byrne in the famous "Big Suit" from the concert documentary *Stop Making Sense*, all twitchy, sweaty, amphetamine energy, would be perfect Pittsburgh weirdos for South Carson Street in the nineties, Butler Street in the aughts or, as I'd maintain, Squirrel Hill at any time. "Pittsburgh reminds me of Baltimore," Waters told *Carnegie Magazine*, "only you have a much better entrance." I take it as a compliment when the artist most identified with Baltimore after Edgar Allen Poe, whose schlock classics *Pink Flamingoes* and *Hairspray* were filmed in his home city, compares Pittsburgh to his beloved urban muse. Byrne, meanwhile, makes his own occasional appearances in the Steel City, even when not touring. Inspired by a group of boisterous Pittsburghers singing him "Happy Birthday" on the event of his turning fifty-two while performing at the Byham in 2004, Byrne took to his bike and explored the city and its attendant mill towns, which he describes in his travelogue *Bicycle Diaries*.

Murray Avenue from the intersection of Forbes— "Upstreet"—the Center of the Universe. *Photo by Jay Dawson, courtesy of* Belt Magazine.

Marveling at the "neighborhoods of immigrant worker housing scattered here and there," with their "local bars, mom-and-pop stores, and pedestrian traffic," Byrne describes hilly Pittsburgh as "beautiful." Traveling to places that you'd expect David Byrne to visit—the Downtown Cultural District, the installation art museum on the North Side called the Mattress Factory—he is amazed by Pittsburgh's reinvention. As he sang on the Talking Heads' seminal 1979 track "Life During Wartime" from *Fear of Music*, "Heard about Pittsburgh, PA?…This ain't no fooling around."

Any city worth the designation "weird" has to have a vibrant art scene that helps makes it so. Both Lawrenceville and Garfield have a thriving scene, the Penn Avenue Arts District going onward for several blocks with small galleries filled with paintings and sculptures created by artists drawn to the city's historically low cost of living. Places like the Wood Street Galleries, the Pittsburgh Glass Center, the Center for Contemporary Craft, the Silver Eye Center for Photography, the Miller Institute for Contemporary Craft and dozens more are a testament to the art scene's energy. None of this is new—for example, the brilliant pop artist and Kutztown native Keith Haring, who combined graffiti, hip-hop and gay culture in his distinctive blocky pictograph figures, which defined the visual idiom of the 1980s, had his first solo exhibition not in New York but rather, in 1978, at the Pittsburgh Center for the Arts when he was only nineteen, having been working there as a janitor before being discovered by the curators.

Surprisingly, the creative firmament in Pittsburgh goes back well into the nineteenth century, for remember that the Queen of the Bohemians, Gertrude Stein, is a native daughter. Also raised in Allegheny City was Mary Cassatt, most important of the American Impressionists, who joined Edgar Degas and Édouard Manet in inventing an entirely new way of seeing the

world, an alchemy of light and color. Cassatt is as canonical a painter as can be mentioned, and yet as is true of all brilliant artists, hers is a vision that works in part because it is weird—that is to say, because it looks at the regular differently. Even though Cassatt is too often dismissed as a painter of "mere" domesticity, she imbues the familiar with the uncanny; she demonstrates to the viewer what is miraculous in the otherwise quotidian. In *The Child's Bath*, for example, an otherwise unremarkable everyday occurrence is elevated to the sacred: the potbellied toddler with fat feet in a blue bowl with a towel draped over her lap, a haggard caregiver in heavy Victorian dress washing the girl, the entire scene only weird in how not weird it is, the artistic equivalent of saying the same word over and over again until it loses all meaning and becomes all the stranger and more beautiful because of it. Then there is Pittsburgh's proletariat painter, the wondrous John Kane: Scottish immigrant, steelworker, railroad painter and celebrant of Western Pennsylvania's charged, numinous power, representing in flat self-taught fashion the skyline of Oakland with the Virgin Mary cradling Christ before the Cathedral of Learning. Similarly in all ways but style, in the twentieth century, the great photorealist Philip Pearlstein rendered sumptuous, massive portraits of nude women and men, presented not as idealized figures but in all their fleshy, splotchy wonder, an evocation of the weird made flesh.

Far more famous than Pearlstein was a friend who also attended Carnegie Tech, an artist named Andy Warhol. If compelled to canonize a saint of Pittsburgh strangeness, then stuttering, aloof, cool, silver-wigged Warhol would be the obvious candidate. Now St. Andy stares out from murals and T-shirts available in his museum's gift shop; there are mugs and posters with that familiar wigged figure sold in bookstores and galleries, even while the poet Peter Oresick wonders in his brilliant *Warhol-o-rama*, "When will you be worthy of my million yinzers?" Ambivalent about his hometown— which returned the favor until more recently, when institutions like the Andy Warhol Museum have started attracting tourists—the Ruthenian, Byzantine Catholic son of a steelworker raised in South Oakland who attended Schenley High School while taking classes at the Carnegie Museum of Art

Opposite: Keith Haring works on a composition in Amsterdam, 1986. *Courtesy of the National Archives in Amsterdam.*

Left: John Kane's 1933 *Pieta*, with the corpse of Christ in front of Oakland's skyline (the Cathedral of Learning only partially complete in the background). *Image courtesy of the Carnegie Museum of Art.*

on Saturdays is almost an exemplary Yinzer. By far the most significant American artist of the second half of the twentieth century, Warhol was a consummately Pittsburgh figure, even if he would have denied it. Part of Warhol's ambivalence was no doubt that when he was growing up, Pittsburgh wasn't the most welcoming to awkward, slight, queer boys, and yet even after having escaped, he remained the everyday Mass-attending son obsessed with the comforts of American celebrity and middle-class consumerism, a working-class kid who moved to New York and named his studio the Factory. What could sound more Pittsburgh than that? Warhol has his moment of affection for the hometown where he would be buried, or at least an imagined moment of affection, in painter Julian Schnabel's 1996 biopic *Basquiat*, when a version of Warhol as played by David Bowie enthuses, "We could go to Pittsburgh! I kinda grew up there. They have this room with all the world's famous statues in it, so you don't even have to go to Europe anymore….Just go to Pittsburgh."

Far more than Warhol, if I had to name a paragon of Pittsburgh weirdness, I'd have to canonize somebody who came close to being an actual saint: clearly, Mr. Rogers. Nobody was more Pittsburgh and also weirder in the most beautiful of ways than Fred Rogers, the ordained Presbyterian minister, jazz pianist and creator and host of the children's show *Mr. Rogers' Neighborhood*, which ran nationally on PBS affiliates for more than three decades. When I say that Mr. Rogers was strange, this isn't a pejorative (as I'd hope would be clear), but there are a few reasons I think that adjective can be applied to him. For one, *Mr. Rogers' Neighborhood* was a

Top: The South
Oakland boy
in Stockholm,
Sweden, 1968.
*Photograph by Lasse
Olson, distributed
under a CC-BY
2.0 license.*

Bottom: Mr. Rogers
with his trolley.
*Wikimedia Commons,
distributed under a
CC-BY 2.0 license.*

gloriously weird show, Zen-like in its simplicity. For more than thirty years, Mr. Rogers would come "home" from some unspecified adult job, switch out of his wingtips into comfortable canvas shoes and trade his sport coat for a cardigan, then prepare his audience for a journey to the Neighborhood of Make-Believe. In an episode, he might discover how crayons or pasta are manufactured or host visitors from the kindly mailman Mr. McFeely to the gruff baker Chef Brocket (the latter a family friend of my parents). In the Neighborhood of Make-Believe there were a variety of characters played by simple marionettes, from the stern autocrat King Friday XIII to the self-effacing Daniel Striped Tiger, brash Lady Elaine Fairchild and wise X the Owl. That all the characters had voices that were a slight variation of Mr. Rogers's own patrician version of the Pittsburgh accent was of no account to me as a child. If anything, it added to the wonderous eccentricity, all of it so obviously the product of its creator's imagination. Another aspect of Mr. Rogers's weirdness that is specific to only Pittsburghers is how we actually did live in his neighborhood. Anyone above a certain age has a Mr. Rogers story about him buying groceries at the Giant Eagle or swimming at the Jewish Community Center. Of course, I've got my own Mr. Rogers story, of meeting him in a long-since-closed camera store on Forbes when I was around sixteen and he was already an elderly man. Nervous to talk to him, I finally introduced myself—hulking and black-clad adolescent that I was— and I informed Mr. Rogers just how much he'd meant to me. And, obviously, Mr. Rogers was every bit Mr. Rogers.

That's the thing that's the weirdest about him—and you can compare anyone's stories: Mr. Rogers really was that kind. And, it should be said, kindness is weird in the most beautiful of ways, because to treat others as the distinct universes that they are—worthy of appreciation, worthy of respect, worthy of love—will always be countercultural in a society configured toward the bottom line; it will always be subversive in a culture that measures humanity by utility. Like St. Francis or Rumi, Mr. Rogers rejected that heuristic. Lest those comparisons seem glib, just turn to Mr. Rogers's contention in his 2002 Dartmouth University commencement address, when he said, "Our world hangs like a magnificent jewel in the vastness of space. Every one of us is part of that jewel. A facet of that jewel. And in the perspective of infinity, our differences are infinitesimal," as apt a squaring of the circle regarding individual singularity and human equality as I've ever encountered. A man of profound faith (he was ordained, after all), Mr. Rogers was never preachy, never sanctimonious. His piety was born from genuine curiosity, a respect that treated everyone equally. This is the

Mr. Rogers who before a U.S. Senate subcommittee in 1969, his remarks commonly understood as being instrumental in saving government funding for public television, said that his purpose was to "give an expression of care every day to each child, to help him realize that he *is* unique. I end the program saying, 'You've made this day a special day, by just your being you. There's no person in the whole world like you, and I like you just the way you are.'" Think about that for a second—in its simplicity, in its tenderness, its empathy, its beauty.

Mr. Rogers's religion wasn't one of bootstrapping individualism, but it did love the individual and the community that could be built between those individuals, the temple of the neighborhood. Friendliness was crucial to his ethic, but more than that, there was the imperative of kindness. Whether assuring children that they couldn't fall down the drain or helping them mourn for a pet fish that had passed away, there was nothing but tenderness, care and love in his perspective. Some reading this chapter may think that starting an essay by talking about furries and ending with Mr. Rogers is meant to be mocking, but I will assure any skeptics that my intent is very genuine and that I see no disjunct here. From Mr. Rogers, we learned that everyone is different, everyone is special, everyone deserves to be loved. The furries, maybe mocked for who they are, maybe scared to be honest wherever they're from, at least for a few days find a home in Pittsburgh, a neighborhood they can call their own. It puts me in mind of a New Year's Eve celebration I attended back in 2017, watching a parade make its way down Penn Avenue with a group of furries waving to the crowd, exhibiting a playful joy that anyone can recognize as such. Right behind them, in the back of an open car and also waving to the crowd, was Mr. McFeely, looking older now, though his blue mailman uniform was as crisp as ever. Weird and beautiful, man.

Chapter 11

THE NATIONAL MONUMENT
TO LABOR SOLIDARITY

A s beloved as the Point State Park fountain might be today, spraying
its 150-foot-high spritz of water gathered from the subterranean
aquifer that is Pittsburgh's quasi-mythic "fourth river," there were once far
more ambitious proposals for how to decorate this rustic space capping the
very end of the Golden Triangle. Both modernist architect Frank Lloyd
Wright and controversial New York City parks commissioner Robert Moses
were hired at different points to propose how to better use the land at the
confluence, with the former suggesting that it would simply be easier to
demolish Pittsburgh entirely—which, at least at the forks of the Ohio, they
did. Derelict warehouses, railroad yards and abandoned factories, as well
as the Manchester and Point Bridges, which once passed overhead, were
all demolished. The Allegheny Conference on Community Development
pushed for this land reclamation; ultimately the development, and others
like it, were the vision of people like Mayor David L. Lawrence, department
store magnate Edgar Kaufman and banking scion and foundation leader
Richard King Mellon, part of a decades-long process that was instrumental
in the city's weathering industrial collapse.

As part of that renaissance, the public-private consortium of Democratic
city government and Republican foundation presidents declared eminent
domain, and since 1974, the area has been a thirty-six-acre state park, with the
outlines of the colonial British garrison Fort Pitt uncovered and highlighted,
as well as the aforementioned fountain. For half a century, Point State Park
has effectively been Pittsburgh's front yard, where citizens enjoy watching

the Regatta on the Allegheny, Monongahela and Ohio or where they listen to performances and peruse exhibits during the summertime Three Rivers Arts Festival. It's easy for Pittsburghers to take perfectly pleasant Point State Park for granted. Perhaps if Wright or Moses had been heeded, there would be stronger emotions about the space, but if any alternative history could be entertained, I most prefer the one where in the city's wisdom, they commissioned Italian sculptor Frank Vittor's 1951 plans for a massive hard-bodied statue of the local folk legend Joe Magarac, rendered in steel (of course) and only five feet shorter than Rio de Janeiro's statue of Christ.

A student in Paris of August Rodin, Vittor was once a celebrated sculptor who was responsible for several public compositions throughout Pittsburgh, most notably the statue of Christopher Columbus near the Phipps Conservatory and Botanical Gardens that has recently been covered in a tarp, but the Joe Magarac statue would have been his most audacious work—in fact, one of the most audacious in civic statuary throughout the United States. The subject of the piece, Joe Magarac, was almost certainly not a real figure. A Pittsburgh Paul Bunyan, Magarac was said to work at the steel mill twenty-four hours a day, finally sacrificing himself within the molten metal of an overheating Bessemer convertor, thus cooling it down and saving his fellow immigrant workers. The earliest reference to Magarac was a 1931 article in *Scribner's Magazine* by Pittsburgh-born journalist Owen Francis, who claimed to have heard legends about the mythic forger of steel from Croatian mill workers who said that it was a popular story in the region. Scholars have since disagreed on who exactly made Magarac up, whether a journalist on deadline invented the "mill hunkie" who could do the work of twenty-nine men or if those "mill hunkies" themselves invented the story over boilermakers of Iron City and Canadian Club when they were being bothered by some snooty *Scribner's* writer.

That the name Magarac means "donkey" in both Serbian and Croatian—with the implication being that he was as "dumb as an ass"—constitutes a clue. Regardless, the mere legend of Joe Magarac is as unreal as the man himself, the story categorized by anthropologists as "fakelore": that is, a supposed myth for which there is no evidence of its existence in oral culture prior to its first written instance. Think of Joe Magarac as a figure from J.R.R. Tolkien but with more kielbasa and pierogies. Despite that, Vittor was taken with Magarac; perhaps, as an immigrant laborer himself, he appreciated the subtle subversions of this prototypically ideal worker who struggles twenty-four hours a day but is dismissed by his fellow workers as a dumbass for having done so. If Magarac was sometimes a

Statue of Magarac formerly featured at the Kennywood amusement park and now in front of Braddock's Edgar Thomson Steel Works. *Photograph by Seth Tisue, distributed under a CC BY-SA 2.0 license. Cropped from original.*

useful symbol for the factory manager, as is evidenced by the statue of him that stands in front of the Edgar Thomson Steel Works, then Vittor's imagination was much more flattering to the workers themselves. Bending an I-beam in his shiny steel hands, the Magarac at Edgar Thomson—which until 2009 was part of a ride at Kennywood—looks more like a goblin than a proletariat superhero. By contrast, Vittor's massive statue of Magarac would have been the most triumphant example of socialist realist art ever to be erected in this nation.

For a minute, envision what the Point would look like if Vittor's proposal had been taken seriously, if wedding parties at the Mount Washington overlook or passengers on the Gateway Clipper could look upon the fourteen-story-tall steel statue of Joe Magarac rather than just the fountain. As rendered by Vittor in sketch and model, the monument would have been framed around a massive sculpture of a shirtless Magarac, the sunset glinting off the metallic shine of the steelworker's muscles, while on either side of the figure there would have been two smaller statues meant to look like cauldrons of molten steel, from which would have emerged a continual waterfall backlit orange to give it the appearance of liquid iron. A 1951 article from the *Pittsburgh Post-Gazette* (without a byline) describes how at the unveiling of Vittor's model, spectators could examine how each "arm of the massive figure would rest on upturned steel ladles, which, in turn, would pour simulated streams of molten steel into a third ladle. That typifies the joining of the Allegheny and Monongahela Rivers to form the Ohio." A 2016 article in *Pittsburgh Magazine* by Virginia Montanez further elaborates on Vittor's design, for as she describes it, the base of the Magarac memorial was to feature forty smaller sculptures, each ten feet high, depicting the impact of industry on the "cultural, social, and business life of the city."

For those who would miss the current fountain, know that Vittor had planned for multiple geysers to be placed around the rim of the entire site, each spraying water almost as high as Magarac himself. As a background, it would make a hell of a prom picture. Hard to say how seriously the city took Vittor's proposal—despite the petition with a thousand signatures of support, my genuine guess is that he had far less of a chance of seeing his vision come to fruition than Wright or Moses did. Most people, as I would conjecture, are probably relieved that Vittor's monument never graced our riverbanks, though the Cathedral of Learning was similarly ridiculous and, I'd argue, similarly beautiful, so I think that Magarac could have been similarly beloved. Acknowledging that I'm in the minority, as many would view the monument as something more fit for East Germany or the Soviet Union, it does make me ask a more fundamental question: Why is there no National Monument to Labor Solidarity? Vittor's sculpture wasn't intended as such—it was probably designed to appeal equally to the boardroom of U.S. Steel and the social halls of the United Steelworkers but there's no reason Magarac couldn't have embodied that lofty purpose, this man who also embraced the most fervent form of solidarity, the most beautiful manifestation of love, when he placed his very body upon the gears to save the lives of those men who worked next to him.

Liberty rises from New York harbor, as she should, for that is a beautiful concept deserving of the monumental. The psychotherapist Viktor Frankl once proposed a Statue of Responsibility in San Francisco Bay to equal out the continent, but that appeals to me less. The National Mall in Washington, D.C., commemorates a multitude of figures, some deserving (Lincoln) and some less so (Washington, Jefferson). What the famously rugged and individualist nation of the United States doesn't have is a National Monument to Labor Solidarity. Though this is a nation which is content to valorize abstract concepts like liberty or individual men we've been told are exemplary, there is no equivalent site (except military memorials) by which we honor those who with broken backs and calloused hands, burned skin and cut flesh, forged the industrial might of this country, in all that is good and bad about that. I wish that at the Point there was a glorious monument, whether Vittor's or not, that honored the organized labor that dug coal, forged steel, laid railroads, canned food, sewed clothes, taught classes, healed the sick, built the United States and made its wealth. Imagine a monument emblazoned in massive, story-high relief with the words of the great Irish-born, Chicago-based organizer of mine workers Mary Harris "Mother" Jones, who in her 1925 autobiography writes, "Pray for the dead and fight like hell for the living!," "The future is in labor's strong, rough hands!" and "Freedom for the working class!"

Sadly, a nation that replaces the beautiful holiday of May Day with the anemic summer's end picnic of Labor Day can't help but find the idea of a monument to the common woman and man anathema, yet it feels as if a tragic lacuna to me. There would be no place more appropriate for such a memorial than Pittsburgh, the city that simultaneously birthed modern capitalism and labor's response to modern capitalism. To be sure, there are any number of industrial sites turned into museums throughout the United States, factories and foundries reconfigured into attractions to educate the populace about the work that once happened (or in some cases continues to happen) there. Pennsylvania alone features the Anthracite Heritage Museum in Scranton; Potter County's National Lumber Museum; the Agricultural and Industrial Museum in York; the Hopewell Furnace National Historic Site; the Dorflinger Factory Museum in the Poconos (dedicated to cut glass); the National Iron and Steel Heritage Museum in Coatesville (near Philly); the Tour-Ed Mine and Museum (featuring a working coal mine), which is just north of Pittsburgh in Tarentum; and arguably the slickest of these institutions, the National Museum of Industrial History (NMIH), an affiliate of the Smithsonian, located in Bethlehem.

That last museum, dedicated on the site of the former Bethlehem Steel plant, was only a few blocks from where I lived for seven years in that eastern Pennsylvania town abutting the border with New Jersey. My apartment window faced the massive, rusting, moon-base glory of the former Bethlehem Steel plant, humungous and looming along the stony banks of the shallow Lehigh River, so that I always appreciated how this small city preserved its industrial history in a manner that Pittsburgh bluntly had not, as we've shunted the ruins of old mills to the periphery of the urban core while paving over Jones and Loughlin or the Homestead Works to build condos and shopping malls. Still, I always had a studied ambivalence about the NMIH, which opened my final year in Bethlehem, despite its clearly well-designed, thoughtful and, most of all, attractive exhibits. Partially, I must admit, it's an issue of civic pride, of Pittsburgh patriotism. Even though Bethlehem was a veritable industrial dynamo that contributed an overt amount to the construction of the modern United States (and I've written glowingly of the city's status in that regard elsewhere), she was no Pittsburgh. It would seem to me that Pittsburgh, not just an iron and steel city like Bethlehem but also a site dedicated to the refinement, production and manufacture of glass, paint, bricks, aluminum, copper, oil, natural gas, cars and food, among other necessities, would be a more suitable location for something named the "National Museum of Industrial History." I'm far from the only person to suggest this; long before Bethlehem was chosen as the site for the museum and before the controversies surrounding its delayed opening, others had proposed that Pittsburgh was best suited and situated for an institution dedicated to industry. In 1982, precisely at the moment the steel industry in Pittsburgh (and later Bethlehem) was imploding, an architecture student at the Massachusetts Institute of Technology named August G. Schaeffer, in collaboration with the Pittsburgh History and Landmarks Commission, submitted a master's thesis titled "Architecture at the Service of Industry: Pittsburgh Industrial Museum—A Design Proposal."

Schaeffer proposed repurposing a series of abandoned railyards across the Monongahela from the Bluff and in view of Downtown as the site for an industrial museum, envisioning this structure as a four-story behemoth with a façade of alternating aluminum, limestone and rusted iron. Writing in his introduction to the thesis, Schaeffer accurately describes the proposed site as

The retired Bessemer converter at Station Square, which functions largely as an antiseptic mall for suburban tourists, gestures toward missed possibilities, as the site could have housed a world-class international museum of industry. *Photograph by Alexander Klyuch, distributed under a CC-BY 2.0 license.*

a "place of raw, natural beauty, which in a curious and poetic way has proved its resilience against the constant development which has taken place there." Featuring an auditorium, a library, several exhibition spaces displaying the thousands of artifacts owned by the Pittsburgh History and Landmarks Commission, as well a massive entrance gallery containing more than a dozen antique railcars, Schaeffer's museum would have been dedicated to an exploration of not just the steel industry but also the entire gauntlet of work that defined Pittsburgh in the twentieth century and, by proxy, would have served as a monument to the entire working class throughout the United States. Such a museum never arose on the Monongahela, though it's true that the Heinz History Museum in the Strip District bears some similarity in both design and mission to Schaeffer's concept.

The most striking aspect of the proposal—and perhaps part of why there is a national museum of industry in Bethlehem rather than Pittsburgh—is in the blunt language that Schaeffer uses to explain the way in which exhibits would focus on those who actually mined the coal and manufactured the steel, describing the institution as focusing on the "brutal working condition for the poor, advancement of laissez-faire capitalism for the rich, and the escalation of America to world power status." Compare Schaeffer's language to the public relations rhetoric on the National Museum of Industrial History's website, which promises to "forge a connection between America's industrial past and the innovations of today by…inspiring the visionaries of tomorrow." The first is resolutely fit for the workers and the labor hall, while the later sounds designed for management and the boardroom. Basing this only on my intestinal premonitions, part of me wonders if such a museum—which required federal funding, after all—was more conducive to Bethlehem than Pittsburgh precisely because the latter remains such a union town. After all, U.S. Steel and the United Steelworkers are both still headquartered right in Downtown Pittsburgh, still only a few blocks away from each other, even if the former's skyscraper is now topped with an ad for one of the new villains of industry, the University of Pittsburgh Medical Center, and the latter is more involved in unionizing hospital workers and adjunct faculty than those who operate the hot metal cauldron. Labor and capital remain a bit too raw to build a Disneyland of industry in Pittsburgh; better to look farther east.

Much of the drama about so-called cancel culture (that is, the pulling down of statues of Confederate officers, the renaming of military bases, the scrubbing of references to genocidal colonizers from national monuments) strikes my Pittsburgh soul as juvenile. Not the pulling down of such memorials (for I see no need to honor Robert E. Lee or Stonewall Jackson) but the reaction of those who claim that this is "erasing history" or disrespectful to the legacy of the past. Juvenile because here in the Steel City, which poet Gerald Stern described as "beautiful filthy Pittsburgh, home / of the evil Mellons," absolutely all of us know what bastards Andrew Carnegie, Henry Clay Frick, George Westinghouse and H.J. Heinz were. Nobody speaks of them with the fantasy fairy-tale logic that demands we pretend that "great" men were good. That's not to say that they don't have monuments; they do. In fact, their names are emblazoned across the limestone of virtually every college, museum and civic institution within the city. But we're also not so foolhardy as to believe any of them to be angels, and we're certainly not offended when the obvious truth that most of them were royal sons of bitches is pointed out to us.

We're grateful for Carnegie's generosity of spirit, which funded our still world-class libraries, less grateful for the fact that none of our great-great-grandfathers could go there to read since they never got any time off (and their union was broken by Pinkertons along the way). Growing up in Pittsburgh, we're always taught the darkness and light, the sweetness and bitter. There are few illusions about the benevolence of the robber barons who forged Pittsburgh. When I was in the public schools learning about the Homestead Steel Strike, nobody would have thought to dismiss it as "woke history"; it was simply history. This is a blue-collar, labor-friendly union town—even still—and we teach our own history. Despite that, however, there is still a Carnegie Museum, a Frick Museum, a Frick Park, a Westinghouse Park, a Heinz Hall, a Heinz Museum, a Mellon Park, a Carnegie Mellon University,

Photograph of the Homestead Steel Works in 1907. *Courtesy of the New York Public Library.*

Entrance to the main branch of the Carnegie Library of Pittsburgh, in Oakland, built in 1895. *Wikimedia Commons, distributed under a CC-BY 2.0 license.*

ad nauseum, but there is no museum or major memorial dedicated to the anarchist organizers of the 1877 railroad strike or the labor leaders like Eugene Debs and Mother Jones whose stories intersected with Pittsburgh's. Even Schaeffer, as radical as his proposal was, highlights the possibility of fundraising campaigns directed toward the copious Fortune 500 corporations headquartered here, and therein lie the reasons for why any institution will tell only part of the story, and a flattering one at that—it all comes down to who pays the bills. Which is why what I yearn for isn't a museum of industry but one of labor, a memorial not to industrialists but to workers.

There are, it must absolutely be said, innumerable individuals keeping labor history alive and several organizations dedicated to those stories. Chief among these is the visionary Rivers of Steel Foundation, which maintains the ruins of the Carrie Blast Furnace, as well as a small gallery at the former Pump House & Water Tower in Munhall and the Bost Building in Homestead, both across the Monongahela and a few miles to the east of where Schaeffer's museum would have been. The foundation directs tours and assembles exhibits, its mission remaining "not simply telling the

An example of the stunning murals painted by Maxo Vanka at St. Nicholas Croatian Catholic Church in Millvale. *Image courtesy of the Vanka Society.*

companies' stories…but the stories of the men and women who worked there." Preserving the remnants of sites and industrial artifacts, Rivers of Steel may promote itself as being involved in "heritage tourism," but it's also very much, admirably, invested in telling a particular working-class narrative too often erased in the triumphalism of civic engagement. As an example, at the time of this writing, the Bost Building is currently displaying a landmark exhibition of work related to the Croatian radical muralist Maxo Vanka, who during the Great Depression would depict Pontius Pilate as a robber baron and Christ as a suffering worker. If ever there was to be a National American Museum of Labor, I'd trust the custodians of Rivers of Steel to maintain it; if ever there was a National Monument to Labor Solidarity, they would be the best people to give tours.

Fairness and propriety necessitate that I must acknowledge those museums and historical sites that, like those maintained by Rivers of Steel, are dedicated to preserving labor history. Youngstown State University's seminal Working Class Studies program hosts a list of just those sorts of institutions, places like the American Labor Museum in Haledon, New Jersey, which preserves the site where striking silk workers met in 1913; the Labor and Industry Museum in Belleville, Illinois; and our own Heinz Museum. There is even the modest but necessary corollary to all those marble mausoleums on the

National Mall in the form of Washington, D.C.'s rarely visited Labor Hall of Fame, assembled by the U.S. Department of Labor and honoring twenty-three luminaries, including Mother Jones. What I imagine, and what I think Schaeffer envisioned, was something more like the People's History Museum in that British steel city of Manchester: a large, modernist building dedicated to not just the elucidation of industry but also the celebration of labor, all of it exhibited in a former hydraulic pump factory that looks more like the Tate Modern than it does a sleepy house in a small midwestern town. The fact remains: in the United States there is no such museum, and there is certainly no major national monument dedicated to the working woman and man.

The American dream was always labor's dream. This dream maintained, though it was difficult and fraught, that honest work meant an honest wage, that in solidarity with other workers you could advocate for your rights, that from your own sweat you could build a comfortable life of improvement for your family and yourself, that your day could be dedicated not just to drudgery but also to yourself. It was a simple dream that gave us vacations and weekends. This was not a dream that was granted; it wasn't conceived on Wall Street or Pennsylvania Avenue but during the Pullman Strike of 1894, the United Mine Workers Strike of 1902, the Steel Strike of 1919, the Textile Workers Strike of 1934, the Steel Strike of 1959. Its Valley Forge and Gettysburg were the Colorado Labor War and the Ludlow Massacre, the West Virginia Coal Wars and Homestead. The armies that took up this banner were the Knights of Labor, the International Workers of the World, the United Steelworkers. That was the past.

Now, two generations of predatory, neoliberal, supply-side, trickle-down, deregulated, privatized, bootstrapping voodoo economics have taken their toll; union membership has long been in free fall, along with wealth for the working class and the American standard of living. "Someone had to be the first," writes Kim Kelly in *Fight Like Hell: The Untold History of American Labor*, "and now the next group of workers who decide to take a moonshot of their own and go toe-to-toe with a giant will get even closer." Today there are new armies, and they've got names like the Amazon Labor Union and Starbucks Workers United. In Pittsburgh, the mills are closed, but the unions remain. Instead of organizing sheet-metal cutters and welders, they enlist baristas, programmers and adjuncts, but the principle remains the same. "It's the constant work of progress and revolution," writes Kelly, "that constant pushing forward, farther, and farther still. It's the unfinished business of centuries of fighters and thinkers and dreamers; each subsequent generation brings us a little bit closer until we can finally see liberation in the distance

Above: Steelworkers demonstrating while on strike in Pittsburgh, 1919. *Wikimedia Commons, distributed under a CC-BY 2.0 license.*

Left: Consortium of labor groups protesting in Pittsburgh in 2022. The demographics may be different, the struggle is not. *Wikimedia Commons, distributed under a CC-BY 2.0 license.*

just ahead." Meditating on what a National Memorial to Labor Solidarity might look like, just go down to Rankin and examine the grand, crumbling edifice of the Carrie Blast Furnace, this Acropolis of postindustrial America. There is a beauty in that massive and ancient place with its rusting blast furnaces and smokestacks silhouetted against an ember-orange sunset the color of molten iron; there is the wisdom that comes with knowing that none of this would have been built but for the hands of the thousands who worked here. As it says above the architect Christopher Wren's grave in his magnificent St. Paul's Cathedral in London, "Reader, if you seek his monument, look around you." Those battles still continue, if not here then elsewhere, unbowed and undefeated.

Chapter 12

HELL WITH THE LID OFF

The description is frequently attributed to Charles Dickens, who did visit Pittsburgh during his antebellum tour, but he wasn't actually the one who envisioned smoky, smoggy, sulfurous Pittsburgh as looking like "hell with the lid taken off." That memorable phrase, oft quoted by Pittsburghers and visitors ironically and not, was actually written by James Parton for the *Atlantic Monthly* in 1868, by which point the city's industry had exponentially increased from where it was decades before when Dickens had spent a day in those soot-coated environs. Parton's infernal quip about Pittsburgh has endured, despite the author himself being forgotten. The reason for that phrasing's memorability is that Parton presents an undeniably arresting tableau, writing about how "there is a street along the edge of the bluff, from which you can look directly down upon the part of the city which lies low, near the level of the rivers. On the evening of this dark day, we were conducted to the edge of the abyss, and looked over the railing upon the most striking spectacle we ever beheld," and from there he spins the six words that for seventeen decades have soldered the image of Pittsburgh as forever drowned in pea-green miasma and gray-slate slag.

"Hell with the lid off" isn't necessarily even the most insulting phrase from the piece; we could have been remembered as the "edge of the abyss." Regardless, that Parton's baroque syntax and Victorian prose remind folks of Dickens is a testament to the *Atlantic Monthly* writer. Unfortunately for us, when Boz visited Pittsburgh in 1842, while on the publicity tour that would end with him writing his single "American" novel, *Martin Chuzzlewit*,

Pittsburgh in 1849, not long after Charles Dickens's visit. *Courtesy of the New York Public Library.*

he was hardly more complementary. A thirty-year-old Dickens arrived down the Allegheny by steamboat to a city of only twenty-one thousand souls, later reminiscing in *American Notes for General Circulation* that "Pittsburg[h] is like Birmingham in England; at least its townspeople say so. Setting aside the streets, the shops, the houses, wagons, factories, public buildings and population, perhaps it may be."

Such a misattribution of Patton's infamous line makes intuitive sense, for Dickens is the great scribe and critic of the Industrial Revolution, the British novelist's prolific output concurrent with the ascendancy of that economic ideology that sees little of sacrificing the environment upon the altar of output and profit. "Smoke lowering down from chimney-pots," writes Dickens in the celebrated first paragraph of *Bleak House*, "making a soft black drizzle, with flakes of soot in it as big as full-grown snowflakes—gone into mourning, one might imagine, for the death of the sun." He's not describing Pittsburgh—industrial London during the Victorian era was muse enough—but it evokes Pittsburgh, written a decade after the author had spent a night by the banks of the Allegheny. Dickens may have snarked on the size of Pittsburgh, but when he visited the city, it was already home to 939 foundries and factories, was a center of the burgeoning rail industry and shipping industry and had become the third-busiest port in the United States and the largest within the interior of the country (it still is, on that last score). By the time Parton visited, Pittsburgh had earned its reputation as Vulcan's forge, Mulciber's foundry, Moloch's factory, for the city had doubled in size and was quickly becoming synonymous with both the delight and degradation made possible by industrial capitalism. By 1911, Pittsburgh had more than half a million people (some ten thousand more than Birmingham), making it the eighth-largest city in the country; far more impressively, the city's mills were responsible for producing 22 percent of steel rails for locomotives, 24 percent of pig iron, 34 percent of Bessemer steel, 44 percent of open hearth steel, 53 percent of crucible steel and an astounding 56 percent of the structural steel used in construction. We had not yet set our record. By the middle of the twentieth century, Pittsburgh was producing more steel than any other city on earth; per capita, more steel rolled out of mills along the Three Rivers than in Birmingham, Manchester and Sheffield combined—more than the entirety of the dwindling British Empire.

Just as the alchemist contemplating a Faustian bargain amid their tinctures and potions faces a mortal risk, so was industrial greatness in Pittsburgh purchased at tremendous personal cost to every person who lived (and lives) within these environs. There is no consideration of what Pittsburgh means without a deep introspection about environmental legacies—in an analytic sense, as well as a more poetic one. At the height of the steel industry (along with all the other attendant industries responsible for the city's wealth and the economic ascendancy), a certain ideology was expressed, an ideology marked by belief that the valuable mineralogical resources studded deep within the crust of the earth are humanity's for the taking, that they can

Pittsburgh seen from Grandview Avenue on Mt. Washington, 1892. *Courtesy of the Carnegie Museum of Art.*

be molded for our benefit in the manufacture of helpful products, which in turn will make a few rich and many middle class. This was the consummate American ideology of the twentieth century, for sure, but stunningly enacted in Western Pennsylvania. Steel mills made Frick and Carnegie wealthy and families named Novak and DiPaolo comfortable, our nonprofit foundations flush with cash, our museums filled with art, our universities filled with students, the homes and apartments of the city filled with people. But the steel mills also cast the sun from the sky, dyed the stones dark and stained handkerchiefs black, made it hard to ever really breath, caused millions of wayward cells deep within the bodies and bones and blood of Pittsburghers to mutate beyond control. This was a city that in the leadup to World War II, before clean air initiatives, was often pitch-black at noon on a summer's day, a place less Dickens's London than Batman's Gotham. A 1906 chamber of commerce report would read, "With the palls of smoke which darken our sky continually and the almost continuous deposits of soot, our dirty streets and grimy buildings are simply evidences of the difficulty under which we labor in any endeavor to present Pittsburgh as an ideal home city."

Half a century after that dismal appraisal of Pittsburgh by its own city fathers, former *Life Magazine* photographer W. Eugene Smith created gorgeous art from the filth in the same way that sand, soda ash and limestone can be pressed into glass. When Smith was asked by author Stefan Lorant to produce a series of pictures for his book *Pittsburgh: The Story of an American City*, it was only expected that his project would take a month. Smith, one of the most talented photographers of his generation, who'd already produced stunning portfolios chronicling the Battle of Okinawa, the work of a country doctor in rural Colorado and Albert Schweitzer's practice in West Africa, ended up staying in Pittsburgh for two years, and rather than producing the agreed-on hundred photos, he delivered to Lorant a stunning thirteen thousand photographic negatives. As an artist, Smith had the eye of an Italian Renaissance painter, a sense of chiaroscuro that made him as if Caravaggio with a camera. *Smoky City*, taken in 1955 or 1956, the original silver gelatin print held by the Carnegie Museum of Art, is a tutorial in Smith's sense of light and dark. Appearing to have possibly been taken from Schenley Park's Panther Hallow Bridge, a preeminent example of the City Beautiful movement of the turn of the previous century, Smith presents a neoclassical landscape framed by the Gothic skyscraper of the University of Pittsburgh's Cathedral of Learning. No detail is visible on that building, however, or on the Catholic Church's diocesan seat of St. Paul's Cathedral, her twin spires punctuating the horizon, for across Oakland's landscape is smeared a thick

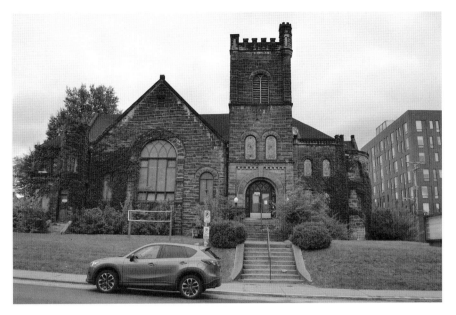

The now-defunct Albright Methodist Church on Centre Avenue. The stones of this heavily soot-stained building would originally have been white. *Photograph by Father Pitt, distributed under a CC1.0 license.*

glop of smokestack black, like a squirt of Jackson Pollock's ink on an abstract expressionist painting. The photograph was taken at noon, but the sky is as dark as night. Smith supplied the consummate document of the United States' environmental degradation in the city that was both most responsible for it and suffered the most because of it. Most disturbingly considering the severity of the picture, at the time that the photograph was taken, Pittsburgh had actually already had a 90 percent decrease in air pollution from a decade before, thanks in large part to the advocacy of New Deal Democrat mayor David L. Lawrence.

This was the Pittsburgh of the first half of the twentieth century, when it was impossible to wear clothing that by midday wouldn't be covered in a thick layer of grimy, black soot. In that Pittsburgh, no surface—homes, businesses, places of worship—wouldn't be dyed black by the smog. In that city, residences required a separate basement entrance (often with a shower and almost always a toilet) so that people wouldn't sully their homes with filth from the mills' exhaust. During the years of big steel's collapse, I recall the university's beautification project in Oakland, the Cathedral of Learning's Indiana limestone sandblasted clean from its previous color of midnight. A reminder is left on the Carnegie Library across the street, one

W. Eugene Smith's
Smoky City, the Cathedral
of Learning and the
twin spires of St. Paul's
Cathedral just barely
visible through the
miasma. *Courtesy of the
Minneapolis Museum of Art.*

divot in its outside wall left its previous color as a token of what the city was like some five decades ago. The house that I grew up in was built of white granite, but it remains black. Western Pennsylvania is where industrial effluent from American Steel and Wire Works was trapped in an air inversion in the Monongahela River so that when the resultant bubble rose to the surface, it suffocated to death nearly a hundred women and men in the town of Donora. In *Devastation and Renewal: An Environmental History of Pittsburgh and Its Region,* Joel Tarr gives a visceral description of Pittsburgh during the halcyon days of several decades ago, describing "flaring of waste gases and columns of black smoke...plumes of white steam that rose as the red-hot coke was cooled....Since the plants worked twenty-four hours a day, these plumes constantly appeared in the visible landscape," where on a "windy day, the odor of sulphur would carry far beyond the mill communities into middle-class neighborhoods." That Pittsburgh remains the Pittsburgh of the American imagination, but decades of legislation and beautification movements have certainly made the city more attractive, even while the pollution has arguably just become harder to see.

The current city fathers might tout a different view from that turn-of-the-century chamber of commerce, one of a Pittsburgh transformed by the "Eds and Meds" of higher education and the health industry, but it's arguably just a less honest appraisal than that of our blunt predecessors. Pittsburgh is more pristine-looking than it was in 1955, but even though we no longer have to wipe the soot from our faces and the dirt from our clothes, that doesn't mean that the city is now a prelapsarian Eden. In terms of short-term particle pollution, we're at number sixteen for metropolitan areas in the United States, and for ozone smog we're at twenty-sixth. For year-round particle pollution (essentially soot), Pittsburgh is the astounding eighth worst in the country, beating out Detroit, Cleveland and notoriously smoggy Atlanta and within a stone's throw of Bakersfield, Fresno and Los Angeles (they're all sunnier, though). The city's abysmal record on pollution is almost singlehandedly due to the output of the Clairton Coke Works, the Edgar Thomson Steel Works and the Irvin Plant, but it's also the legacy of the still underexplored environmental degradation of almost two centuries that has poisoned air and soil while leading to this area having the third-highest incidence of cancer in the United States, where half of the residents know somebody who has died of the disease and an astounding 20 percent will ultimately succumb to it. I would need three hands to count the number of friends I've known who while in their twenties or thirties would have to bury a parent who died of cancer. My own father passed from a rare form of blood cancer half a decade ago. At least a quarter of the homes on the idyllic street that I grew up on have been similarly affected by whatever is in our air, our soil, our water.

There is a global cost as well. "We have hastened the end of the Holocene Era, which endured over the last ten thousand years," writes Steven Best in *The Politics of Total Liberation: Revolution for the 21st Century*, "which endured over the last ten thousand years, and thereby have precipitated the arrival of the Anthropocene Era—whose very name proclaims our global dominance and the severe environmental impact of *Homo sapiens*." The Anthropocene is an evocative term coined by ecologists to describe how humans are capable of altering the very geology of the earth in a manner once reserved for asteroids and volcanos, plate tectonics and axial spin, how the fruits of our industrial civilization are toxins in the soil and holes in the ozone, plastics in the ocean and carbon dioxide in the atmosphere.

What the Anthropocene means is flooded cities, billions of refugees, failed crops and resultant famines, increased pandemics, intolerably high temperatures and, finally, ecosystem collapse. From the tilled soil of

Left: Pittsburgh blast furnaces at night, as represented in a woodcut from the cover of *Harper's Magazine*, 1885.

Opposite: A gushing oil well in the appropriately named Oil City, site of the first drills in history, from 1899. The oil is gone now, but natural gas still remains. *Courtesy of the Library of Congress.*

industrial capitalism grows the tree of apocalypse. Now, instead of plague, famine, war and death, the Four Horseman of the Apocalypse are joined by (as Best enumerates them) "extinction…resource scarcity, global capitalism, aggressive neoliberalism, economic crashes, increasing centralization of power, rampant militarism, chronic warfare, and suffering and struggling everywhere"—and more than anything, by anthropogenic climate change. Scientists debate when exactly the Anthropocene began, though most naturally posit it as starting with the Industrial Revolution, the toxic child of the nineteenth-century reaching maturity now. If Pittsburgh had an outsized role in industrial history, then by definition, it has a responsibility in the dawning (and maybe dusk) of the Anthropocene. By 1850, Western Pennsylvania was the leading miner of anthracite coal; a hundred miles north of Pittsburgh was where the world's first commercial oil well went into production in Titusville, Pennsylvania; today an astounding 177,000 natural gas wells operate across the commonwealth. All of this is intrinsic to climate change, whether in the nineteenth century or today: trillions of tons of carbon dioxide expelled into the air, raising the average temperature catastrophically at an exponential pace. Gas, oil, coal—the detritus of extinct animals getting their ironic revenge during the current biosphere collapse.

So that aforementioned ideology that Pittsburgh's industry represented mid-century becomes even more complicated beyond the scope of the painful personal repercussions it has had for those of us living in the region. Pittsburgh's ideology represented work, labor, industry, capitalism, wealth, but it's only fair to admit that these fantasies have been apocalyptic. That's not to blame Pittsburgh or, certainly, Pittburghers at all—far from it—only to suggest that if Pittsburgh (and Detroit, Cleveland, Flint) represented an industrial dream, we now better understand how we're waking to a nightmare. Blaming Pittsburgh alone for the Anthropocene would be insane, of course—there have been many Pittsburghs: Birmingham, Sheffield and Manchester; Cologne, Dusseldorf and Essen; Magnitogorsk, Novosibirsk and Chelyabinsk; Guangzhou, Qingdao and Shenzhen; Jubail, Riyadh and Jeddah; Detroit, Cleveland and Flint. All of them have contributed, and still contribute, to the ongoing and oncoming ecological calamity. All of them are parents of the Anthropocene after their own way. But as we are among the earliest and the largest, our name reserves the right to a bit of that sulfury Armageddon. Not that our contributions to climate change are merely historical, for just as pollution endures in Pittsburgh, so does heavy industry churning out carbon dioxide. A 2023 survey by the group Penn Environment found that half of the heaviest emitters in the commonwealth are in southwestern Pennsylvania, with the Edgar Thomson Steel Works—founded by Andrew Carnegie in 1875—among the top five worst, a complex opened only seven years after Parton's hellish observation that's still

poisoning our air and heating our planet. Pennsylvania is the fourth-worst state in terms of contributing greenhouse gases, of which 44 percent of that carbon dioxide is supplied by the Pittsburgh metropolitan area. In a single year, Penn Environment reports, over ten million metric tons of that greenhouse gas is produced by only two corporations: CONSOL Energy and U.S. Steel.

"We're rallying here just a few miles from where the corporate robber barons have settled down to divide up the planet," shouted Ashley Smith through a bullhorn on the granite steps of the City County Building on September 24, 2009, "that group of bankers, financiers, and political leaders who have wreaked havoc upon the world." An editor for the *International Socialist Review*, Smith demanded that the crowd "fight for another world, put people before profits." Smith, a Vermont-based activist, was addressing a gathering called the People's March, a motley assortment of environmentalist, anarchist and socialist activists that had descended on Pittsburgh after it was announced that the city would host the G20 Summit on Financial Markets and the World Economy. Even though I'd taken part in the massive protests against President George W. Bush's invasion of Iraq only half a decade before, spending several minutes chanting in front of Carnegie Mellon University's portion of the military-industrial complex in the form of the glass-clad fortress of the Software Engineering Institute, I took a more skeptical view of groups like the local Thomas Merton Center, Code Pink, the Woman's League for Peace and Freedom, the Socialist Workers and Pittsburgh G20 Resistance.

On the evening of September 25, with more sanctimony than self-awareness (though a bit of both), I posted on Facebook that the "response about the G20 protesting has been fascinating. All of the Pittsburgh people (and as you may know, we have a visceral connection to our hometown) have been primarily disgusted with the protesters." Despite standing by the window in the cool air-conditioning of my apartment some eight stories high while watching a line of helmeted and armored police walk as a phalanx toward unarmed protesters clad in black bandanas and ripped jeans, regardless of my having read about the several thousand law enforcement officers who had also descended on Pittsburgh to use tear gas and an experimental "sound cannon" on those same protesters, my civic empathy apparently didn't extend to the folks marching against the machinations of the world's most powerful human beings gathering Downtown, because all of my feeling was subsumed in the travesty of a brick being thrown through a Starbucks window or some graffiti on the side of the Apple Store. "Ah, but I was so much older then," sings Bob Dylan on his fourth album. "I'm younger than that now."

There was a pride when President Barack Obama selected Pittsburgh for the G20, sandwiched as we were between conferences held in London and then Toronto. At the surprise announcement of the conference's location, Obama touted how Pittsburgh had "transformed itself from the city of steel to a center for high-tech innovation—including green technology, education and training, and research and development." Obama selected Pittsburgh

Riot police at the Pittsburgh G20 in front of the County Building. *Wikimedia Commons, distributed under a CC-BY 2.0 license.*

Protestors in Lawrenceville during the 2009 gathering of the G20. *Wikimedia Commons, distributed under a CC-BY 2.0 license.*

after security concerns precluded New York, where the conference was supposed to coincide with the opening of the United Nations General Assembly, and so in a short amount of time, plucky little Pittsburgh prepared for the arrival of the twenty most powerful people in the world. With only four months' notice, Pittsburgh hotel rooms hosted people like French president Nikolas Sarkozy and German chancellor Angela Merkel, King Abdullah bin Abdul Aziz of Saudi Arabia and Prime Minister Gordon Brown of the United Kingdom.

Arguably no event had made Pittsburgh so visible in so many nations as the G20. Local media was delighted—less so regarding the arrival of the activists, as even my largely leftish coterie of colleagues and friends, associates and family took a jaundiced view of the protesters, born not from their politics but a provincialism that desired Pittsburgh not be embarrassed in the international media. In a moment of more introspection, I asked on Facebook, "If this were happening in Washington, and we were watching it on TV, I wonder if we would be more sympathetic to the protesters?" I can answer that from experience, for when I actually was living in Washington, D.C., during the street battles that followed George Floyd's murder, when the then-current president took advantage of the District of Columbia's strange federal arrangement and declared martial law, effectively occupying the capital with National Guard troops from mostly deep red southern states, I had nothing but sympathy for the protesters, and in that circumstance, I joined them. After all, as Dylan sang, "I'm younger now."

We all are. If the entire global situation seems different a decade and a half later, so then does the local situation. Pittsburgh's selection for the G20 was another accidental gift to then-mayor Luke Ravenstahl, only twenty-six when he assumed office following the tragic sudden death after a short cancer illness of the popular Mayor Bob O'Connor. Taking the oath with a tremendous amount of popular goodwill, Ravenstahl—widely regarded as a bit of a moron—quickly squandered it through innumerable stupid scandals. His successor, City Councilman Bill Peduto, was elected as a liberal in the Obama mode, but over the eight years he was in office, he governed essentially as the representative from Walnut Capital, a friend to developers more than the populace. If Peduto was a young, exciting firebrand in 2014, then by 2022, he was an ossified relic of a Democratic Party machine who cheaply accused his primary opponent Ed Gainey—who would go on to be elected the city's first Black mayor—of being a "socialist." Peduto would distinguish himself as the first incumbent in city history to lose, despite

Left: French president Nikolas Sarkozy and his glamorous first lady Carla Bruni arrive at a gala held in the Phipps Conservatory and Botanical Gardens. *Wikimedia Commons, distributed under a CC-BY 2.0 license.*

Right: Then Russian president Dmitri Medvedev, an obvious proxy for Vladimir Putin, arrives at the Phipps with his wife. *Wikimedia Commons, distributed under a CC-BY 2.0 license.*

winning in 2017 with 96 percent of the vote. In the interim, all of us had been mugged by reality.

The doctrine of everything being fixed with development, the utopia of craft breweries and shopping malls on slag heaps, had little to offer in the way of actual ideas facing the current crisis. We'd all experienced the rise of right-wing authoritarianism, the increase in political violence, the COVID-19 pandemic, and it demanded a genuine response. Comparing 2009 to today, Pittsburgh announces itself as a far more left-wing city, a place that would stand with the marchers rather than those gathered in the convention center. The Democratic Machine has unraveled, as not only do progressive figures like Gainey get elected but the city also sends to Congress Summer Lee, the first Black representative from Pennsylvania and a leftist in the mold of Alexandria Ocasio-Cortez. If the Pittsburgh doctrine was one that lent itself to the Anthropocene, I wonder if the solutions to those problems might be found here, if the organizers of the G20 were correct about our fabled resiliency but if it might manifest in a surprising way.

Fifteen years after the Pittsburgh G20, I'd argue that that conference was a surreal introduction to our current world, that our contemporary situation established itself on the streets of the city, which the activists themselves understood. When Obama announced Pittsburgh as the location for the conference, his tone was in keeping with the optimism of his campaign, where despite the collapse of industry, our future was a bright, technocratic, progressive one based in compassionate free market principles. That this very model of neoliberalism increased inequity, without even cleaning up the environmental degradation of the previous decades, escaped me. Sandwiched between the 2008 bank collapse, which saw none of those responsible punished in any significant way, and the aborted promise of the Occupy Wall Street movement, the Pittsburgh G20 was an interregnum in which the current moment was made manifest.

More telling, as if the foreshadowing of a novel, was the guest roster of leaders. Turkish prime minister Recep Tayyip Erdoğan, already in office for six years and still in office as I write now, spoke at the David L. Lawrence Convention Center, as he was already in the

The People's March on Grant Street. *Wikimedia Commons, distributed under a CC-BY 2.0 license.*

midst of constructing a novel form of illiberal democracy that sheathed fundamentalist beliefs in the trappings of modernity. Silvio Berlusconi, prime minister of Italy, enjoyed a dinner of hydroponically grown vegetables at the Phipps Conservatory, regarded as a comical buffoon by the national media of both our country and his own, even as his borderline fascist politics prefigured the rapid descent toward authoritarianism that has marked the past decade. Standing atop Mount Washington, espying the autumnal oranges and red of Pittsburgh in September, was President Dmitri Medvedev of Russia, the hand-chosen puppet of Vladimir Putin, some thirteen years before the genocidal invasion of Ukraine, of which he remains a vociferous advocate.

No major decisions came out of the Pittsburgh G20—not really. No real commitment to transitioning from fossil fuels, no actual promises to reduce carbon dioxide, no genuine seriousness about tackling climate change. Just lots of bromides about the new economy, encomiums to technology, pretty stories about a bright future and the resurgence of forgotten places. Regardless, for a weekend, the whole future as it would actually occur was here. For a bit—in all its coming darkness. The solution to the crisis of the Anthropocene was demanded by the protesters I saw marching down Centre Avenue—it wasn't in the convention center but outside of it.

Chapter 13

ONLY PITTSBURGH IS
MORE THAN PITTSBURGH

In the deep-grooved and often rainless valleys of the Central Pangean Mountains, beneath the shadows of tropical peaks that despite being bisected by the equator were still capped by snow as they ascended heights of thirty thousand feat, the fin-backed mammalian-amphibian Edaphosaurus, which measured an impressive fifteen feet in length, would have made its barrel-chested, bow-legged perambulations through forests of fern that were incapable of decomposing, as fungi hadn't evolved yet. Three hundred million years ago, during the earliest years of the Permian Epoch, the Edaphosaurus perhaps gathered in packs, animals not of the hills but of mountains. The steep jaggedness of this range was formed when the North American, African and European continental plates crashed together, generating a line of mountains that ran as if the massive sail on Edaphosaurus's back, from the neck of Pangea to its tail. Across that world primeval traipsed a panoply of exotic beasts that joined Edaphosaurus, such as the gargantuan but stubby pug-faced, frog-like Eryops and the winged reptile Weigeltisaurus, who would glide through the thick atmosphere above freshwater rivers in which the slick-webbed Hynerpeton swam, a multitude of massive arthropods and aquatic invertebrates marking the flora and fauna of this deeply alien realm. "No birds winged through the…swamps," notes a decades-old marker at an exhibit on the Permian at the Carnegie Museum of Natural History, "because birds would not evolve for another 100 million years." In a poetry that paleontologists and geologists are fluent in, the display notes, "Only the rustling of the leaves, the hum of the wings

Edaphosaurus. *Wikimedia Commons, distributed under a CC-BY 2.0 license.*

of giant dragonflies—the largest insects that ever lived—and the scurrying sounds of giant cockroaches and centipedes could be heard."

Almost a hundred million years later, erosion and entropy had buffed the peaks of the Central Pangean Mountains down to a low roll, across which stalked the three-toed dinosaur Grallator, who only announces his existence to us in footprints. Twenty years ago, a set was discovered in Vale of Glamorgan, Wales, which appeared almost identical to those found in 1933 while historians were excavating at the Gettysburg Battle Site. The reason for the commonality was simple: Grallator had much less distance to traverse when the Allegheny Mountains and the Welsh hills and Scottish Highlands were all of a single range. Long before Scotland gave Pittsburgh its accent, they shared the same mountains, and it's the exact same veins of coal that run underneath Pennsylvania and Wales that were mined from the earth. Officially purchased from the Seneca in 1768, the Pittsburgh Coal Seam below Western Pennsylvania and West Virginia has produced—from the ossified bodies of creatures like the Eryops and Edaphosaurus—the deposits that would be burned for fuel, that would be used in the production of coke and the smelting of iron and steel. From coal came gold; from those fossils came riches.

Mysteriously, it was almost as if the original settlers to Western Pennsylvania were somehow involved in suturing together those landmasses that had drifted apart hundreds of millions of years ago, believing that they had traveled thousands of miles only to have never even really left their homes. They may have unconsciously believed it was a blessing; maybe it was a curse. Such are the strange poetics of place, the ways in which the land itself can't be gotten away from. Where once Edaphosaurus and later Grallator lived and died, now there are white-tailed deer, coyotes, bobcats and black bears in the Appalachians; puffins, red deer and highland cattle in Scotland; the Barbary leopard and lion in the Atlas Mountains of Morocco. The austere, jagged, tan Highlands, the unforgiving, blistering, red-sandy heat of the Atlas, the low undulation of the Alleghenies: all were the same range but separated eons before the dinosaurs because of the relentless machinations of continental drift.

"the appalachian mountains are older than saturn's rings," tweeted librarian @bookishseawitch late in 2022 in a post that went viral. "the appalachian mountains are older than dinosaurs. the appalachian mountains are older than trees. the appalachian mountains are literally older than BONES." Written in the characteristic online prosody that at its best evokes modernist poetry, @bookishseawitch's thread has the admirably quality of being both scientifically accurate and hauntingly beautiful. Every single observation made in her tweet is empirically verifiable: dinosaurs emerged 228 million years ago, trees first evolved 360 million years ago, Saturn's rings are 400 million years old, which is the same age as the earliest animals with bones, but the Appalachians arose an astounding 1.2 billion years ago. The Appalachians, and by transitive property the Alleghenies, are among the most ancient features on the face of this planet; to live in such a place, to be born here, work here, die here—there is something strange, uncanny and beautiful in that. There is a mystery in such mountains; they exist beyond mere meaning. So often, paeons to place focus on that admixture of the geological and the anatomical, the way in which people are impacted by the features of a landscape, but the Appalachians—this ancient, mystical place—are so old that they predate not just our bones but the very idea of bones.

Geology has a wisdom that's so deep and wide and expansive that it's insulting to even call it wisdom; such anthropomorphism means nothing when facing the unfathomable age of something like the hills on which Pittsburgh would be one day built and the hills on which Pittsburgh will inevitably one day disappear. A wisdom that by definition is chthonic.

Knob Mountain in Western Pennsylvania. Once it would have been taller than the peaks of the Himalayas are today. *Wikimedia Commons, distributed under a CC-BY 2.0 license.*

The course of the Youghiogheny and Monongahela, the Allegheny and Ohio, will deviate, their banks will flood and face draught, but the hills will remain, slowly eroding as they have from that epoch well over a billion revolutions of the Earth ago in which they were taller than Everest. Today technology and mass media conspire to grant us the illusion that we're "free" from landscape, that every place is effectively the same as every other place, because the supercomputers that we carry in our pockets imply that it is so, but the mountains do not let you forget that they are not the same as every other place. "The bird's-eye view is not ours," writes the geographer Yi-Fu Tuan in *Space and Place: The Perspective of Experience,* "unless we climb a mountain."

My initial writing about my hometown, at least when I began formally being published on the topic, broached an argument not much more complicated than "I'm from Pittsburgh and I would like to be paid for writing about being from Pittsburgh." As is the want of the vocation, oftentimes an argument presents itself to you not when you've decided to work on a project but through the process of reading, researching, thinking and, most of all, tackling the writing itself. Like a scene emerging from a developing photograph, whatever your claim might happen to be arises out of the chemical reactions of your research and work, of your

Western Mountain in Columbia County, Pennsylvania. *Wikimedia Commons, distributed under a CC-BY 2.0 license.*

subconscious rumination on these things. For me, consistently, what I've always returned to is the *landscape* of Pittsburgh. What I have to argue is far from academically incontrovertible; it is not necessarily rigorous, scholarly, analytical, empirical, objective, scientific, historiographical or unassailable by the boring dictates of peer review. What it happens to be is something that I deeply know not in my bones but in my mountains, which are older than bones—that this ruptured, craggy, hilly, chasm-crossed, steep, inclined and beautiful place in all its danger and absurdity is mystical— enchanted—numinous—both immanent and transcendent—as well as sacred—precisely because of the landscape that has deigned us worthy to build our city and towns upon it, for a bit at least. More important than the paint has always been the canvas. Naturally, when living on a billion-year-old hill that was once Himalayan, the mind turns toward the subject of permanence. What will Pittsburgh be, not in a billion years but in the coming century, at least? After our brief role as less-than-perfect stewards of this landscape—extracting that mineralogical wealth from the crust and forging it into metal, while growing rich and sick at the same time—do we have anything to offer the wider world, or is our fate to recede, to disappear as one of those many once-important places that obscures into myth or, as is worse, mere nostalgia?

Brian O'Neil, in the essay from *The Paris of Appalachia* that I quoted in the introduction to this collection, claims that part of Pittsburgh identity is to be defined by the fact that our greatest days as a city are most assuredly behind us, the better to embrace a stoic quietude. That makes a particular intuitive sense; often, maybe even most of the time, I'm in complete agreement with him. Sometimes I'm not totally sure, though—not exactly positive that our most important days are behind us. In this, the hazy days of the Anthropocene that we did so much to bring about, I wonder if there are years of redemption ahead of us, if perhaps Pittsburgh might not offer a model, perhaps even a haven and a refuge for a small portion of this overheating planet? Demographically, as has been discussed repeatedly throughout these pages, Pittsburgh suffered a calamitous population decline, but I suspect—actually, I'm certain—that this city will not just be larger in the future but also, possibly, the largest it's ever been in its history. And not just us but also our sister Rust Belt cities such as Cleveland and Detroit, all of them suddenly attractive as the Southeast and Southwest become intolerably hot and dangerous, as the coasts flood and overcome New York and Boston, Los Angeles and San Francisco.

The Allegheny River frozen over in the winter. *Wikimedia Commons, distributed under a CC-BY 2.0 license.*

These industrial midwestern metropolitan areas all have easy access to the globe's largest reservoirs of fresh water in the form of the Great Lakes, so much so that some demographers have begun to refer to the region as the Water Belt. According to journalist Juliette Rihl in the nonprofit newspaper *Public Source*, Florida State University sociologist Mathew Hauer has predicted that climate refugees from both the coasts and the South will contribute over two hundred thousand people to the population of Pennsylvania. "Pittsburgh fits the climate haven profile," writes Rihl. "It has relatively cool average temperatures, a relatively low risk of natural disasters and certain infrastructure like roads, bridges and rail lines were built to accommodate a much larger population." In models of the severe effects of climate change, Pittsburgh fares well, largely insulated from the worst possibilities of hurricanes and cyclones, tornadoes and wildfires, with the biggest change to the weather locally being increasingly severe summer thunderstorms and an average temperature that will evoke Atlanta or Miami. Still, it will be livable. In fact, maybe Pittsburgh will finally, de facto, embody its claim to being the "most livable city" in the nation. A number of other experts have posited Pittsburgh as being among the most likely to endure the increasingly dire climate catastrophe, despite our pollution and outdated infrastructure. Logan Sachon and Pat Howard—writers covering the insurance industry for *Policy Genius* and thus the true prophets of our age—rank Pittsburgh as the eighth-best place to endure climate change. As the authors note, historically, "the city is resilient."

Pittsburgh over the next fifty years could see itself double, or even triple, in population as climate migrants from the coasts and the South move here, attracted to the relative safety of the mountainous clime, what Jeffrey Fraser in *Pittsburgh Quarterly* describes as a "shelter from the storm." Some Rust Belt cities already have dedicated offices to planning for the presumed influx of internal refugees. That has yet to happen in Pittsburgh, but in both the media and informally in local government, you begin to hear discussion of a question that once seemed not just unthinkable, but borderline absurd: What will we do with a potentially exploding population? Absurd because we've taken senescence as our legacy for nearly two generations now, the assumption being that there are never new Pittsburghers, only former Pittsburghers. Yet the census shows that not only has population loss in Allegheny County stalled, but the number of new residents has actually been (slowly) increasing.

Anecdotally, Pittsburgh itself has seen a number of new residents from both the politically deep red environs of rural Pennsylvania and from red states that are enacting draconian laws that violate the civil rights of already marginalized communities. As the city's local government and its populace become increasingly progressive, Pittsburgh announces itself as a Mother of Exiles standing tall above the flooding embankments. We've had a long history of immigration to Pittsburgh, from the waves of arrivals from eastern and southern Europe to internal refugees during the Great Migration. All of that is a complicated history, of course, so that the question now must be if we'll embody the best of that welcoming legacy rather than the worst. When considering the vagaries of geology, what is so crucial to remember, again, is the longevity of this landscape, its role as nourisher and protector but also as an often dangerous realm that is much bigger and more ancient than us. The Central Pangean Mountains are not unrelated to Pittsburgh's future status as a climate refugee destination—in fact, they're intrinsically connected. The former is the only reason why the latter is the case. There will be flash flooding, there will be landslides, there will be the haze of distant wildfires (there already is). The city will be hot and humid, and storms will rage, but hurricanes won't have the same energy as on the coasts, and derechos will be slammed into pieces by the undulation of these cool mountains that we live on, those once gargantuan peaks rubbed close to the earth but still close enough to heaven so as to shroud us in a security that perhaps even Edaphosaurus felt. Deep history is in the land; it's the only poetry commensurate with eternity.

"A community is the mental and spiritual condition of knowing that the place is shared, and that the people who share the place define and limit the possibilities of each other's lives," wrote the ecological philosopher and writer Wendall Berry in *The Long-Legged House*. "It is the knowledge that people have of each other, their concern for each other, their trust in each other, the freedom with which they come and go among themselves." Community is a reminder that the land has never been ours, that we're only of the land, for a bit—and most important, that our status as Pittsburghers is neither intrinsic nor essential to ourselves but that it's in our commitment and our love of this place, something that anyone, anywhere can choose for themselves. There is, as I've written earlier, what the Romans called the genius loci, a "spirit of place," that connects the profane realm with something numinous. Any place that is a billion years old perhaps has this tinged sacredness about it, this transcendent enchantment. Our greatest bard, Jack Gilbert, wrote a line that perfectly encapsulates the miracles encountered here, noting in the *American Poetry Review* that *"only Pittsburgh is more than Pittsburgh."* What a cracked axiom, what a bizarre principle! Yet completely true! My suspicion

The furnaces of the world are now burning about 2,000,000,000 tons of coal a year. When this is burned, uniting with oxygen, it adds about 7,000,000,000 tons of carbon dioxide to the atmosphere yearly. This tends to make the air a more effective blanket for the earth and to raise its temperature. The effect may be considerable in a few centuries.

Above: A 1912 issue of *Popular Mechanics* predicts climate change and educates its audience by using a picture of a Pittsburgh steel mill.

Left: W. Eugene Smith's photograph of Pittsburgh's Dream Street. *Courtesy of the Carnegie Museum of Art.*

is that those who've never been to Pittsburgh would dismiss Gilbert's turn of phrase as nonsensical, at best a tautology and at worst a paradox, but in either circumstance effectively meaningless.

Ask a Pittsburgher, however—whether young or old, new or established— and they'll understand how the electric convulsion of this place is such that everywhere else can seem prosaic, how even our self-hatred is a form of love and that a crackle of static and spark of molten iron still permeates this town even though the mills are long shuttered, because it was never the work that we did but the land on which we did it that mattered. How only Pittsburgh is more than Pittsburgh in the same way that adding infinity to infinity still gets you infinity. *How adding nothing to infinity still gets you infinity.* "We die and are put into the earth forever," writes Gilbert, saying that "we must insist while there is time. Must eat / through the wildness of the sweet body already / in our bed to reach the body within that body," which is immaculate Pittsburgh thinking. The transitoriness and fallibility of our small human lives, the permanence of the earth on which we live, the physicality of the transcendent and the wisdom of the body. Driving around the steep wooded corner and seeing those glass and iron and steel towers erupt again from the very ether, always as if you're seeing them for the first time; the wide and tall and deep and broad shape of the landscape with its hills and mountains plunging toward its rivers, the earth forever there even as we fade away, the otherworldly genius of a land older than the bones in our bodies—which lets us grace it for a time—listening to the dull hum and ecstatic hymn of the summer crickets and always, always, always the sound of a train in the distance.

Conclusion

AND NOW, SQUIRREL HILL

W hen a gunman entered the Tree of Life Synagogue on October 27, 2018, and murdered eleven women and men, I was not living in Pittsburgh. By that point, I'd lived away from Pittsburgh for eight years, in eastern Pennsylvania, New York City and then Massachusetts. I'd still live away from my hometown for another three years, for a bit in Washington, D.C., and then in northern Virginia. Regardless, as soon as I heard about this tragedy, this bloodletting, this nightmare, I knew that I would return to Pittsburgh, that I would make it my home one day once again. It was inevitable.

In the hours after the first frantic texts, the continual doomscrolling, the frenetic movement of the cable television chyron, I became intimately familiar with the concept of "neighbor." During this time, I reconnected with people that I hadn't talked to in decades, people who shared the same indescribable feelings that I did, but at the same time, I also lost contact with friends not from Pittsburgh who didn't understand those same feelings. Perhaps uncharitably, I had a rage at not being contacted by some, of not hearing inquiries about how I was doing, how my community was doing. Such a reaction couldn't be helped. There was an anger that I had—at the monster who committed such an atrocity, surely—but also those who reduced the neighborhood of Squirrel Hill to this violation, to this interloper who invaded and killed. People I knew with the barest connection to Pittsburgh used the tragedy for social media cachet, the mass media descended and did what they always do, politicians sent senseless thoughts and prayers, always the thoughts and prayers—and all of it was impossible for me. I needed to be in Pittsburgh.

The house in which I grew up was exactly a mile from Tree of Life. When I was in high school, friends and I would spend time playing pool in the youth lounge; I'd attended bar mitzvahs there, holidays there. Part of the uncanny horror of such a thing is to see the name of your home become a symbolic stand-in for the worst thing that ever happened there. There are award-winning documentaries and books on that hideous day; one account is named after my neighborhood. I'm sure that these works deserve their accolades, I'm sure that they're thoughtful and important, but I've never watched or read them, and I'm not sure that I'll ever be able to. The distance of a mile is too short. Now I live only a few blocks from the synagogue, and I'd never want to live anywhere else.

Too many Americans, unfortunately, know what it means for their community to be the victim of hideous mass gun violence (and if they don't, they will). Nobody with my last name can ever be totally unaware of the ugly endurance of anti-Semitism; I had nightmares while growing up that what did happen, would happen. Yet there is a subtle distinction between being surprised and being shocked. What happened here—the largest pogrom in American history—was a Jewish tragedy, an American tragedy, a Pittsburgh tragedy. The rabbis speak of something called *tikkun olam*, of healing the world. Everyone has their role in that task; since I'm a writer, that's how in my own infinitesimal way I try to suture up the wounds of this fallen world, at least a bit, a stitch at a time. About an hour or so after I first heard the news, in my apartment looking out at the flat marshlands of Boston with the Prudential and John Hancock Buildings rising up from the Atlantic, I quickly wrote the following piece. When I first began this book, I knew that I had to end with Squirrel Hill, and I thought that I'd edit and revise this essay to update it, but I think in its immediacy and directness, it still says everything that I'd ever want it to say.

OCTOBER 27, 2018

An eruv is normally a thin line of metal wire that stretches across the tops of telephone poles, barely visible to an observer who doesn't expect it, looking scarcely different from the normal infrastructure that you would see in any large city—perhaps a line to bring cable television into homes. But the purpose of an eruv is different: rather, it serves to encompass a Jewish community entirely within a symbolic border, whereby private and public domains are blurred and it becomes possible for Orthodox Jews to carry whatever needs to be carried outside of their literal homes on both the Sabbath and Yom Kippur, the Day of Atonement.

In Pittsburgh, the eruv encircles almost the entire historically Jewish neighborhood of Squirrel Hill, as well as Greenfield, parts of Regent Square and Point Breeze, where I grew up. It runs down Forbes Avenue, past verdant Frick Park and the Victorian mausoleums of Homewood Cemetery; it runs alongside porched homes on South Braddock Avenue and by the edge of the Parkway East; it briefly runs parallel to the meandering, brown Monongahela River and snakes up Browns Hill Road; to the west, it briefly dips into Schenley Park past college students playing frisbee or sunbathing (depending on the season), and it traces back around Wilkins Avenue. This thin wisp of ephemeral wire turns what is public into a common treasury—it converts an entire community into a home. More than that, it functions as a membrane, as a skin, binding neighbors together as one body. A few hours ago, somebody whose name doesn't deserve to be mentioned pierced that skin, walking into the Tree of Life Synagogue on Wilkins Avenue with an assault rifle and killing at least eleven congregants. I still don't know who among the dead I might know.

One of the largest urban Jewish neighborhoods outside of the New York metropolitan area, the community is home to dozens of synagogues across the entire theological spectrum, from small Hasidic shuls to massive Reform temples, from liberal Reconstructionist communities to modern Orthodox congregations. One of the city's largest and most diverse neighborhoods, it's always been a haven for immigrants, from the burgeoning communities of Chinese, Korean and Vietnamese who have opened up restaurants and shops that line Forbes Avenue and the long crooked, cement-cracked spine of Murray Avenue to Middle Eastern immigrants who, in the years before Pittsburgh's Muslim community would grow large enough to support halal markets, would do their grocery shopping at Kosher Mart.

Bordering both Carnegie Mellon University and the University of Pittsburgh, the neighborhood has always been an intellectual's paradise, the sort of place where homes are stuffed with an ungodly number of books and where the Carnegie Library is among the most frequented in the entire commonwealth. Squirrel Hill tolerates idiosyncrasy, uniqueness, oddness. Wandering the blocks of the central business district are scores of characters, dreamers and schemers, scores of delightfully weird and open people. This was the location of the Presbyterian Church that Mr. Rogers, an ordained minister, would preach at. This is where Hasidic families walking to shul on Saturdays wish each other a "Gut Shabbos," something that owes more to

Crown Heights then it does to the Midwest. Squirrel Hill is exemplary of America, of the best of the country. Which is why as our nation cannibalizes itself in a nightmare of fascistic hatred, it was the locus of this evil act.

Such is the continual nightmare of this American bloodletting, this "American carnage," these horrific, dark, exhausting, terrible, hellish atrocities visited upon our communities every single day. Too many of you reading already know what it is like to see your towns, your neighborhoods, your cities profiled on television and the Internet after such hell has been visited upon them; too many of you know the surrealism of seeing those places that you love suddenly plastered across media because of the actions of evil men. And many of you who do not understand it inevitably will someday, and for that I am heartbroken. And for that I am angry.

That Jews were the target of this person's delusional rage is not surprising, at least not to anyone who has paid attention to both the vagaries of history and the hateful rhetoric that permeates our discourse right now. This is not an issue of "civility" or of "Both sides are responsible." No, I feel completely entitled to examine the poisonous fruit of our current political culture and to rightfully accuse those who now occupy the highest positions of power and influence in our nation and to point to them as being those who are responsible for sowing such discord. Every anti-Semitic dog whistle, every hateful meme, every manipulative conspiracy theory promulgated by the current administration leads a path to what happened in Squirrel Hill today. But that man who occupies the White House, that thing who can't even utter condolences without blaming the victims whose blood is still warm—*that man does not deserve to have every single story be about him*. So, content in knowing his responsibility, I will not mention him again here.

Because Pittsburgh—*Pittsburgh is blessed*. And Squirrel Hill—*Squirrel Hill is blessed*. So today, we say a *baruch* for Pittsburgh, for Squirrel Hill. We think of hanging out with friends in the dwindling twilight of a June evening on Forbes Avenue, eating Italian ice and seeing the sun reflected off the tops of distant skyscrapers. We think of the winding cobblestone streets snaking up the hill, and we think of mighty sand-colored synagogues that dwell at their tops as if golems surveying their villages. We think of pastrami at Rhoda's, pancakes at Pamela's, cheesesteaks at Uncle Sam's, cheesecake at Gullifty's, pizza at Mineo's, midnight breakfast buffet at Eat'n Park and Iron City at the Squirrel Cage. We think of the boys in their black hats and the girls in their long skirts trailing behind them as they walk to yeshiva. We think of the Hebrew letters on the clock set in its tower at the JCC looking over the intersection of Forbes and Murray, and we think of creased used paperbacks by I.B. Singer and Joseph Roth purchased at Amazing Books or Classic Lines. We think of the triumph in vinyl in the rows of Jerry's Records, and we think of Christmas Chinese food dinners at How Lee or Chengdu. We say kaddish for those we lost: for wives and husbands, for sisters and brothers, for mothers and fathers, for daughters and sons. For friends. But we need not say kaddish for Squirrel Hill, for she is still there.

Squirrel Hill will always be my home, and my heart will always be in Squirrel Hill. When I was a teenager, my friends and I used to hang out "upstreet" on Forbes and Murray after school ended, incongruously grabbing cheesesteaks as Shabbos would begin in the early descending sunsets of winter. There was a period when we took to wishing each other a "Gut Shabbos" on those Friday afternoons, and though Judaism was not a tradition in which I was raised, I was irresistibly drawn to this ritual, not just because of the sense of community that it offered but in the mystical apprehension that the Sabbath could be as a world unto itself, a utopia of not space but of time. In much medieval Jewish poetry, the Sabbath is presented as a queen, who ushers in a brief kingdom that is as a respite from the horror of this world. The modernist poet Hayim Nahman Bialik, in imitation of those Hebrew, Yiddish and Ladino lyrics, writes in a poem that the "sun has already disappeared beyond the treetops, / Come let us go and welcome the Sabbath Queen, / She is already descending among us, holy and blessed, / And with her are angels, a host of peace and rest."

Today I think of a different poem, by Pittsburgh and Squirrel Hill's native son the great Gerald Stern, who in his lyric "The Dancing" records his family's reaction to the end of the Second World War. He writes that he never "heard Ravel's 'Bolero' the way I did / in 1945 in that tiny living room / on Beechwood Boulevard" (which intersects Shady Avenue only a block away from Tree of Life). Stern writes that he never "danced as I did / then...doing the dance / of old Ukraine" for "the world at last a meadow, / the three of us whirling and singing, the three of us / screaming and falling, as if we were dying, / as if we could never stop" here "in Pittsburgh, beautiful filthy Pittsburgh." The wisdom of "The Dancing" is the wisdom of the Sabbath, that even in the midst of such pain, sorrow, heartbreak and evil, there is still the respite of that sacred day, when we sing a prayer of both the "God of mercy" and of that "wild God." Auto-da-fé could not abolish the Sabbath, nor could pogrom, nor gas chamber, nor bullet. As I write this, it is still the Sabbath. And a week again, there shall be another one. And the week after that, it shall come again. Forever, both here and in Squirrel Hill and everywhere else where people are still capable of love.

ABOUT THE AUTHOR

Ed Simon is the editor of *Belt Magazine*, an emeritus staff writer for *The Millions*, a monthly columnist for *3 Quarks Daily* and a staff writer for *LitHub*. He holds a PhD in English from Lehigh University and has taught writing at several institutions of higher education, most recently at Carnegie Mellon University. Simon is a frequent contributor at several different outlets, including articles at the *Atlantic*, the *Paris Review Daily*, *Aeon*, *Newsweek*, the *Washington Post*, the *Los Angeles Review of Books* and the *New York Times*, among several others, and his work focuses on questions of religion, literature, faith and their discontents. He is the author of several books; his most recent titles include *Relic*, part of Bloomsbury Academic's Object Lessons series; both *Pandemonium: A Visual History of Demonology* and *Elysium: A Visual History of Angelology* from Abrams; and *Heaven, Hell and Paradise Lost* from Ig Publishing. In the summer of 2024, Melville House will release *Devil's Contract: The History of the Faustian Bargain*, the first popular, comprehensive cultural history on that subject. He has written about his hometown before in *An Alternative History of Pittsburgh*.